A PICTORIAL HISTORY OF
NORTHWEST AIRLINES

A PICTORIAL HISTORY OF
NORTHWEST AIRLINES

by Stephen E. Mills

BONANZA BOOKS • NEW YORK

This book was originally published under the title
More Than Meets the Sky.

Copyright © MCMLXXII by Superior Publishing Company
All rights reserved.

This edition is published by Bonanza Books,
a division of Crown Publishers, Inc.,
by arrangement with Superior Publishing Company.
a   b   c   d   e   f   g   h
BONANZA 1980 EDITION

Manufactured in the United States of America

Library of Congress Cataloging in Publication Data

Mills, Stephen E
    A pictorial history of Northwest Airlines.

    Bibliography: p. 189.
    Includes index.
    1. Northwest Airlines, inc.—History.
I. Title.
HE9803.N65M53   387.7'065'73   79-25560
ISBN 0-517-30999-8

DEDICATION

To the men and women, past and present, who contributed to the founding and growth of one of the world's most successful airlines:

FOREWORD

Every effort has been made to do justice to the history of Northwest Airlines in honor of its 50th anniversary. A complete record of this pioneer airline would require volumes if it were to include the many thousands who contributed to the growth of the company and if it related the many worthwhile accomplishments and unbelievable experiences. My apologies in advance to those of Northwest's over 20,000 past and present employees who inadvertantly have been omitted; time and space dictates that your participation — your stories as well as many facets of the industry — are encompassed in those of your co-workers who have been mentioned.

In the hundreds of interviews unselfishly granted to me, it is gratifying to note that without exception every individual expressed the same pride of association with Northwest Airlines — in many cases an entire working life in esteem of employer and profession.

Northwest Airlines is an outstanding member of commercial aviation, which is the newest segment of the transportation industry; a fraternity that has developed in an accelerated atmosphere of expensive progress and fierce competition.

Gratitude is expressed to Mr. Donald W. Nyrop, president of Northwest Airlines, to the home office staff, the air crews and support personnel — oldtimers and newcomers — who cooperated to the fullest extent in assisting me in my writing task. No one coached, dictated or demanded; one Northwest veteran stated, "Write the story as you see it, Mills, we stand on our own landing gear!"

Famous aviation pioneer and Northwest Airlines' career pilot Walter R. Bullock reminisces of old Northwest Airways days with Captain Vince Doyle, Northwest Airlines' pilot and historian. Bullock, who joined Northwest September 1, 1927, was the nation's youngest licensed pilot when he learned to fly in November, 1916, at age 17. Retiring from the company March 15, 1961, Bullock keeps active in aviation building, rebuilding, repairing and flying antique aircraft. On May 12, 1972, he received one of the nation's highest aviation honors when he was inducted into the OX-5 Club of America Hall of Fame. Twin Cities based Doyle skippers a Boeing 747 pictured on wall behind.

ACKNOWLEDGMENT

A large degree of credit resulting in this publication is cheerfully extended to Vince Doyle, who, unselfishly and without compensation, enthusiastically made my task a relatively easy one by supplying hundreds of photos, publications, covers and other material. Also, my thanks to him and his lovely wife, Barbara, for providing my "home away from home" while researching in the Twin Cities area.

My sincere appreciation to Doyle, Ron Stelzig and Jim Borden, who, from start to finish, spent untold hours advising, editing and proof reading — a great team.

Additionally, rare photos and important information were generously contributed by R.C. "Andy" Anderson, Robert Bates, Hart and Lucille de Mers, Jack Deveny, Norm and Dorothy Hilsen, Mrs. Croil Hunter, William A. Kidder, Joe Kimm, C. W. "Nippy" Opsahl, John Vars and Bill Wallace.

For granting extensive and engrossing interviews contributing greatly to the text and photo clarification: Hal Barnes, Walter Bullock, Barbara Doyle, Al Henderson, Harold Hodgson, Earl Hohag, Frank Judd, Lou Koerner, "Donnie" Lavery, Carl Magnuson, Tom Nolan, Bill Richmond, W. E. "Red" Slaughter and Art Walker.

A special thanks to Dick Allen, Howard Barron, Sherman Booen, Roland W. Chambers, Jim Dilonardo, Frank Ernst, A. E. Floan, Jim Freeburg, Bill Hamilton, A. B. "Cot" Hayes, Tom Hillis, Leo Holt, Jack Malone, Harry McKee, Ted Tax, Giles Velte, R. Charles Velte and Gordon Williams for advisement on various technical and factual segments.

For invaluable assistance and excellent cooperation, my thanks to the public relations department: Roy K. Erickson, vice president; Walter Hellman, manager; and Carol Larson, secretary.

Additional appreciation is extended to R. L. Towne, director-external relations, McDonnell Douglas Corporation; Dexter Cushing, public relations, Boeing Company; Darold Harris, dispatcher, Nezperce National Forest; Jack R. Hughes, general manager, Johnson Flying Service; Bob Reeve, president, Reeve Aleutian Airways; and Albin C. Hammond, air operations, Region 1, U.S. Forest Service.

Lastly, my thanks for assistance given by historian-writer James W. Phillips for consultation and editorial advisement; my wife, Pat Mills, for manuscript typing; Sheri Howard and Ione Steen for overall reading.

All photos not otherwise credited were furnished by Northwest Airlines and Vince Doyle.

Twin Cities-Chicago air mail pilots at Speedway Flying Field, Minneapolis. On fuselage, from left to right, are E. Hamilton Lee, H. F. Smith and L. H. Garrison. Front, standing: H. C. Starkey, W. L. Carroll. K. M. Stewart and Burr H. Winslow are behind them on struts of the DeHavilland twin-engine piloted to Minneapolis from Chicago by Lee on November 7, 1920.

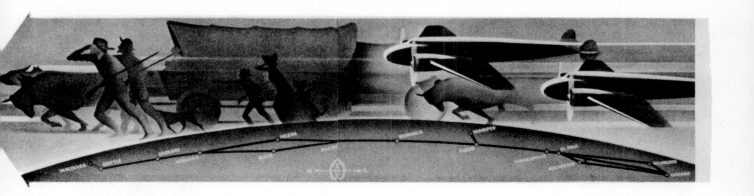

TABLE OF CONTENTS

Chapter 1 – AIR MAIL ROUTE NUMBER 9

The history of Northwest Airlines is one of pioneering over rugged mountains and vast oceans. It chronologs the transition of a small, regional air mail carrier to an international airline. Northwest Airways was an outgrowth of earlier general aviation events which evolved Northwest Orient Airlines into its present stature.

After that historic day on December 17, 1903, at Kitty Hawk, North Carolina, when Orville Wright made the first powered flight, the first commercial flight of any importance was in September, 1911, when mail was carried by air from Garden City, N.Y. to Mineola, L.I., a distance of six miles as a one-week experimental venture.

The outbreak of World War I and the ensuing rapid technical development of aircraft produced a surplus of aircraft and experienced pilots. The United States Post Office Department in 1918, following a brief air mail experiment by Army service pilots, availed itself of both men and equipment to establish the first effective air mail service.

Commercial aviation per se was established in 1926, when the United States Congress passed the Air Commerce Act and created the Aeronautics Branch of the Department of Commerce. Air mail routes formerly flown by the Post Office Department were turned over to commercial operators on a contract basis.

Prior to this, and while still under the auspices of the Post Office, the first transcontinental air mail route was established September 8, 1920 from New York-Chicago-San Francisco. Soon afterward, feeder lines were augmented to the main route. One of the first opened was between Twin Cities-Chicago on August 10, 1920. The base of this operation was a wooden hangar at Speedway Field, later named Wold-Chamberlain Field, and now known as Minneapolis-St. Paul International Airport.

Ex-army pilots and mechanics flew surplus twin-engine Martin and DeHavilland bombers, single-engined DeHavilland DH-4s, Hisso Jennys and Standard biplanes, in an effort to meet the daily round-trip schedule. A total of eight planes were lost and four pilots killed during this difficult nine-month operation and service was discontinued June 30, 1921.

No further attempt was made to revive air mail service on the Twin Cities-Chicago route until aviation enthusiast Charles "Pop" Dickinson secured an air mail contract in March, 1926. With three Wright J-4 powered Lairds, an open cockpit biplane built by pilot Henry C. Keller and a cabin plane built by pilot Elmer Partridge, Dickinson commenced operations on June 7, 1926, per contract requirement. The first day the weather was adverse and one of his pilots, Elmer Partridge, was killed shortly after takeoff in a crash south of Minneapolis.

In March, 1926, just prior to Dickinson's establishment of his Minneapolis-based line, airportless St. Paul purchased the site of the present municipal airport (now known as Holman Field). Three months later, the city — largely through the joint efforts of Col. L. H. Brittin, at that time vice president of the St. Paul Association, and William A. Kidder, early aircraft dealer and charter service operator — passed a $295,000 bond issue to develop the field. The new field was visited in August by a regional tour of Ford Trimotor and Stinson airplanes sponsored by the Ford Motor Company and called the Ford Reliability Airplane Tour. This event stimulated local interest in the airfield and awakened the city to the fast growing potential of aviation.

Following one month of hardship and missed schedules, Dickinson filed the required 90-day notice of suspension of operations, putting him out of the contract October 1, 1926. The visionary Col. Brittin wanted in. He enthusiastically, but unsuccessfully, negotiated with National Air Transport, Robertson Aircraft Corporation and Stout Air Service endeavoring to finance and establish an airline to replace the Dickinson line. With time running out for pickup of Dickinson's contract, Brittin next consulted Kidder in an effort to raise the money, as the pair had been deeply involved in promoting the St. Paul airport bond issue. On an invitation from Henry Ford, Kidder and Brittin went to Detroit and met with 30 prominent automobile industry people at a Detroit Athletic Club luncheon. When the meeting ended in the

Opposite: Charles "Pop" Dickinson, first Twin Cities-Chicago air mail contractor, is shown at the nose of one of his Laird Whirlwind biplanes with a mechanic and Eddie E. Ballough, right, Dickinson's personal pilot and later a noted circus and race flyer. Dickinson, a pilot himself for 20 years up to the time of his death, succumbed to a heart attack in 1935 at the age of 77. Other Dickinson pilots were Nimmo Black, William S. Brock, Daniel Kaiser, Henry C. Keller, Al Sporrer and Elmer Partridge.

cigar smoke-filled room, the necessary capital had been pledged.

With 29 Detroit and St. Paul stockholders holding $300,000 in par value certificates, Northwest Airways, Inc., a Michigan corporation, was organized in August, 1926. Officers of the new company were: Harold H. Emmons of Detroit, president; Col. L. H. Brittin of St. Paul, vice president and general manager; Frank W. Blair, president of Union Trust Co. of Detroit, treasurer; William B. Stout, president of Stout Air Service, Detroit, secretary. Original members of the board of directors were: Eugene W. Lewis and E. S. Evans of Detroit; J. M. Hannaford, Jr. and Robert B. Shepard of St. Paul.

On September 4, 1926, Northwest Airways was awarded the Post Office Department air mail route number nine contract, Twin Cities-Chicago, for a sole bid of $2.75 per pound. The second oldest air carrier in the United States with single continuous identification began operations October 1, 1926.

Noted race and stunt pilot Charles W. "Speed" Holman was named first pilot with David L. Behncke and Robert W. Radall as pilots. Andrew J. Hufford was chief mechanic and Elmer F. Leighton, mechanic. November, 1926 personnel further included A. K. Grant, mechanic; Julius Perlt, clerk; and George O. Miles, chief clerk. Two rented aircraft, an OX-5 Curtiss "Oriole" and a Thomas-Morse "Scout," served as equipment. During the latter part of the same month, three new Stinson "Detroiter" cabin planes were purchased and went into operation November 2, 1926, carrying air mail only. On July 5, 1927, the first passenger service was inaugurated on the Twin Cities-Chicago route; $50 one-way.

The fledgling company became the first airways in the history of transportation to coordinate air-rail service when it began working with the Great Northern, Northern Pacific, Milwaukee and Pennsylvania railroads in August, 1928. This service included transfer of passengers and express freight from trains to planes and vice-versa. For the most part, Ford Trimotors and Hamilton single-engine all metal monoplanes were used as equipment.

In December, 1928, Northwest inaugurated the Fox River Valley route with air mail service to Milwaukee, Fond du Lac, Oshkosh, Appleton and Green Bay, Wisconsin.

Company records indicate that between October 1, 1926, and June 24, 1929, Northwest planes flew 908,264 miles of regular transport operations. During this period, 187 emergency landings were made due to adverse weather, four due to engine trouble, and 12 for miscellaneous reasons. With the addition of charter and taxi flights, the complete distance flown for that period totaled over 1,000,000 miles.

In May, 1929, control of Northwest Airways was purchased by Twin Cities capital and administrative headquarters were established at the Merchants Bank Building in St. Paul. The officers of the company were: A. R. Rogers, chairman of the board of directors; Richard C. Lilly, president; Col. L. H. Brittin, vice president and general manager; H. C. Piper, vice president; Julian B. Baird, secretary-treasurer; C. A. Gunderson, assistant secretary-treasurer. Members of the board of directors were: Hon. Frank B. Kellogg, Roger B. Shepard, F. T. Heffelfinger, J. M. Hannaford, Jr., H. R. Weesner, L. J. Shields, R. R. Rand, Paul J. Kalman, G. Nelson Dayton, George K. Gann, R. F. Pack, William B. Mayo, C. D. Johnson, Col. Paul Henderson and Earle H. Reynolds. Operations manager was Charles W. Holman, traffic manager C. G. Chadwick, and business manager J. H. Cooper. Chief pilot was Chadwick B. Smith, chief engine mechanic Andrew J. Hufford and chief aircraft mechanic James B. La Mont.

In 1929, Northwest Airways was among the first to uniform their flight crews and adorn the navy blue uniform with the new Post Office Dept. official air mail wings, designed by Col. L. H. Brittin, and still worn proudly by NWA pilots.

By 1930, the company had enjoyed a fantastic growth throughout the greater Minnesota area. In March of that year, service was extended to Rochester and passenger and express service was begun between Madison, Wisconsin, and Chicago, Illinois, via Janesville, Rockford and Elgin, Wisconsin. Service was extended to Beloit in September.

Northwest Airways' general office was established in St. Paul's new $100,000 terminal building in July, 1930. Hangar and service facilities at Minneapolis' Wold-Chamberlain field were expanded and incorporated passenger waiting rooms.

By the end of 1930, company officials under the tireless leadership of Brittin, reincarnated the pioneering spirit of Lewis & Clark by trail and James Hill by railroad, and cast their eyes on new routes to the west.

Two famous early-day aviation figures appear in the photo at left. Standing at right is Col. Louis H. Brittin, founder and for many years vice president and general manager of the then Northwest Airways. Standing left is William B. Stout, first secretary of the airline and a noted aircraft designer and engineer. Seated left is Frank W. Blair, vice president, and at right, Harold H. Emmons, first president of Northwest. It was under Col. Brittin's energetic and farsighted leadership that the small airline emerged in the early 1930's as one of the nation's major air carriers.

Gold-winged OX-5 Curtiss Oriole shown below is one of two and eventually three aircraft leased by Northwest to begin operations. This ship was owned by William A. Kidder, owner of Curtiss Northwest Airplane Company. Kidder, an aircraft dealer and early aviation enthusiast in the Twin Cities area, has been quoted as saying that a few quick brush strokes on his sign and Northwest Airways was in business. The second aircraft leased was an OX-5 Thomas-Morse. The third ship was used only briefly before Northwest took delivery of their new Stinson Detroiters. Kidder photo.

Charles "Speed" Holman, left, noted stunt and race pilot, is shown in photo at right with photographer T. K. Kelly, center, and his employee, right. Original Northwest wooden hangar in background frames Holman's Laird LC commercial biplane before it was converted to a speed-wing and the registration number was changed to R 7087. Despite Holman's exhibition flying, as Northwest's first operations manager he was an astute businessman and is credited with the success of all the early-day flying aspects of the company. His black Laird often carried the name or emblem of Northwest Airways. Photo furnished by Mrs. Charles W. Holman.

Left: Original home base for Northwest was this wooden hangar at Wold-Chamberlain Field.

Late in 1926 Northwest purchased three new Stinson Detroiters, one of which is shown at right in the building process. Col. Brittin, right, persuaded builder Eddie Stinson, center, to move Northwest's order ahead of the others with compensation to the earlier purchasers. The Detroiter, designed by Stinson, was so named because it was financed by a group of Detroit businessmen. It was the first closed-cabin aircraft ever used by a commercial airline. At left is William Mara, chairman of the Mayor's Aviation Committee of the City of Detroit. Workman is unidentified.

16

Rare photo at right is of Northwest's Stinson Detroiter No. 2 after being placed into service, sans registration numbers. It was during this period of time that registration numbers were being required by the U.S. Department of Commerce. Painting on the numbers was a gradual process and first compliance usually appeared prefixed by the letter "C". Robert Bates collection.

Mrs. George E. Leach, wife of the mayor of Minneapolis, christens one of Northwest's three new Stinsons in photo below. Joining in the late 1926 ceremonies are (L-R) David Behncke, one of Northwest's first pilots and later the co-organizer and first president of the Air Line Pilot's Association (ALPA), the pilot's union; William A. Kidder, aviation pioneer; James Lincoln, Minneapolis Association of Commerce, and William Stout.

Dave Behncke, left, assists Major R. W. "Shorty" Schroeder of the U.S. Department of Commerce, center, and Col. L. H. Brittin with an inspection of the first Stinson to arrive in the Twin Cities area. This Detroiter, ship No. 2, was flown by Behncke from Detroit. Ship No. 1, flown by "Speed" Holman and Ship No. 3, flown by Eddie Stinson, left the industrial city at the same time but encountered a snow storm west of Milwaukee and were forced to turn back. Note temporary Northwest emblem on fuselage side. Schroeder, a former military pilot, applauded Northwest on their choice of aircraft.

17

Photo above, taken inside Northwest's old wooden hangar at Speedway
Field, Minneapolis, in late November, 1926, is one of the entire company
flight operations personnel. From the left, Bob Radall, Elmer Leighton,
Dave Behncke, Col. Brittin, "Speed" Holman, Earl Allred, A. H. Grant,
Andy Hufford, George Miles and Julius Perlt. Below is reproduction of
Northwest's payroll voucher for November, 1926; a total expenditure of
$838.43.

Although Northwest Airways began operations October 1, 1926, it did not carry its first passenger until July 5, 1927, On that day, Byron G. Webster, then a St. Paul laundry executive, climbed into the cabin of a Stinson "Detroiter" at the St. Paul airport and landed at Chicago — a distance of 360 miles — 12 hours later. In 1927, Northwest carried 106 customers before passenger operations were suspended for the winter. Note "signature of agent" in lower left corner is that of Col. Louis Brittin, general manager and vice president.

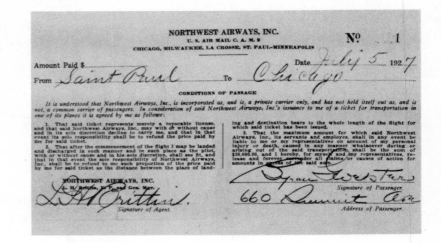

Left: Modernized fleet of Stinson Detroiters appeared in plumage of gold wings, gold striped black fuselage and first appearance of famous Northwest emblem. Paint chipping on cowling resulted in burnished natural aluminum finish. Note metal propeller sans spinner of earlier photos. The Stinson carried three passengers and cruised at 85 mph. Northwest purchased a total of four of these aircraft, the first closed-cabin planes used by a commercial airline.

Right: Speedway Field, Minneapolis, as it appeared about 1928, was originally owned by Guy Thomas of that city. Barney Oldfield and Eddie Rickenbacker were among drivers who participated in the only 500-mile race staged over the wavy two-mile concrete course September 4, 1915. The ill-fated track area reverted to farming. Hangar at right center was built by the city and leased free of charge to the U.S. Post Office during the 1920 air mail flights. On July 22, 1920, four DH-4 DeHavillands on the U.S. Army New York-Nome, Alaska flight stopped at Speedway Field. Over 100 aircraft appeared at the 1923 dedication as an airport and in 1926, Speedway Field was named Wold-Chamberlain Field. Hangars built in 1921 in right background were base for famous Minnesota National Guard 109th Aero Squadron. The track, for years a landmark, later required heavy blasting to remove portions of it.

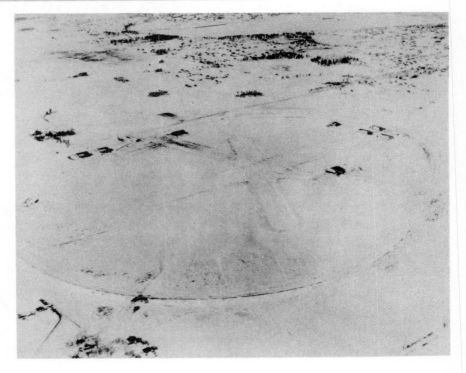

HAMILTON
METAL PLANE

Left: A total of nine 7-passenger Hamilton "Metalplanes" were eventually flown on Northwest routes; the second plane to be delivered is shown the winter of 1928 at Wold-Chamberlain Field. The first Hamilton, NC 7523 (No. 20), was destroyed by fire February, 1933. The Metalplanes, built in Milwaukee, Wisconsin, boasted of cabin heat and toilet facilities. The 550-hp Hornet powered aircraft served Northwest well for over nine years.

Bob Gilsdorf, Clara Wanvik, Ruth Conrad and John Vars with pilot "Speed" Holman demonstrate Northwest's new airliner ease of entry. Leather coat and goggles worn by Holman were standard attire for all company pilots. Extreme cold winters in open cockpits demanded this protection. Holman apparently is taking no chances on the advertised Hamilton cabin heaters.

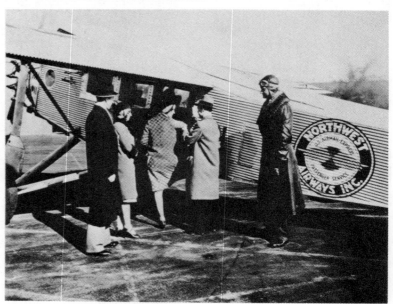

Below: On September 1, 1928, the first coordinated air-rail service in the history of transportation was started by Northwest Airways. This operation was under the regulations of a technical committee headed by Col. Charles A. Lindbergh; the service included passengers as well as express.

FORD TRIMOTOR

The Ford Trimotor "Tin Goose," introduced to the air traveling public in 1928, was the first "large" commercial air transport of all-metal construction. In the fall of that year, Northwest took delivery of the first two of a fleet of five Fords. Shown in photo above is NC 7416 and Company No. 30, a model 5-AT-A, ship No. 5-AT-2, which was the first Ford of that series to be sold to a commercial airline. Ford NX 6926, often erroneously shown in photographs with Northwest markings, was the first of the series and sold to Pratt & Whitney Aircraft Co. NC 7416 was lost in a crash at St. Paul in June, 1929. Photo by J. E. Quigley.

Left photo of Ford interior which boasted of "windows that open and close and complete lavatory facilities." Metal seats shown here replaced earlier wicker type. Earphones were installed on this flight for passenger enjoyment of commercial broadcasting. AM radio head can be seen in bulkhead above. Note heater registers in the aisle.

The Standard Ford 5-AT model sold for $55,000 and was equipped with the new and powerful Pratt & Whitney 420-hp engines. Payload was increased to 12-14 passengers depending on the cabin configuration. Below photo of NC 7739 is the second Ford purchased by Northwest and is Company No. 31. Both Fords were placed on the Twin-Cities-Chicago route. The word "Ford" painted on the vertical stabilizer was ordered removed from all the ships by Col. Brittin. "Ford doesn't own them anymore," he was quoted as saying. NC 7739 was destroyed in a 1930 Chicago hangar fire. Hilsen Collection.

December 15, 1928, Northwest extended air mail service to the Fox River Valley in Wisconsin. Pilot L. S. "Deke" DeLong, who flew the inaugural flight, is shown in above photo in air conditioned cockpit of ski-equipped Waco 10W, equipped with Wright J-4 engine, receiving a mail sack from postman at Green Bay. The aircraft, which is Company No. 5, had a factory list price of $7,215 — less propeller.

Left: Before takeoff on the first night air mail flight from Twin Cities to Chicago the summer of 1929, pilot "Deke" DeLong shakes hands with George Drake, Minneapolis assistant postmaster, from the cockpit of his Waco. C. L. "Les" Smith flew the westbound flight. Hilsen collection.

In photo below, Northwest Airways' agent Leo Torson prepares to load mail sacks into Waco piloted by Mal Freeburg for night flight.

In 1929, Northwest was among the first airlines to uniform their personnel. In photo above, attired not quite so stylishly by today's standards but just as skilled are (L-R) Homer Cole, Jack Malone, Walter Bullock and Fred Whittemore. The traditional wings worn on the left breast were added later. Pilots wore six-button coats while non-flying employees wore those with four buttons.

Below: 1929 route map. The Twin Cities-Rochester-Chicago route was served by the Ford Trimotor "The Gray Eagle." The "Silver Streak" Hamiltons and "Blackbird" Stinson Detroiters were flown on the Twin Cities-LaCrosse-Madison-Milwaukee-Chicago line.

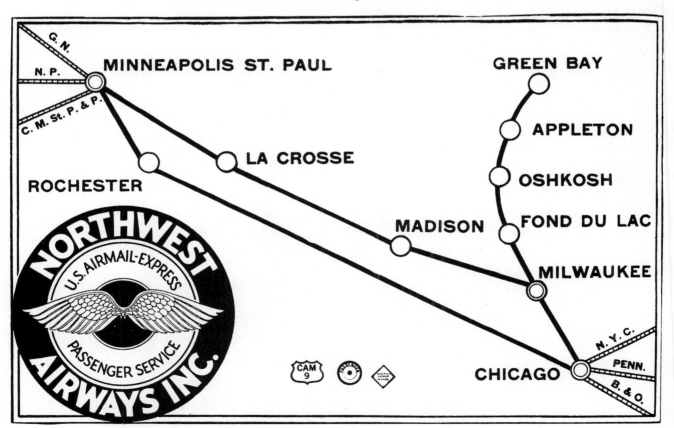

Above: These are some of the pioneers who helped build Northwest Airlines into one of the world's major domestic and international airlines with a route system stretching half way around the globe. Top row, from left: Homer Cole, Fred Whittemore, Chad Smith, Charles A. "Speed" Holman, Walter Bullock, John Malone, Joe Ohrbeck. Center photo, standing, from left: M. E. Andersen, unidentified, Hank Aune, Al Haulson, Walt Reed, Chet Brown, Martin Leadon, Ben Foster, Al Opsahl, Oscar Knudson, Miles Cooper. Center picture, sitting, from left: Ted Anderson, Ray Maher, Ted Hallin, Bill Hoffman, Clarence Opsahl, Lou Koerner, Tom Hillis, Leo Holt, Jack Noble, Charles Potter. Bottom row, from the left: Mel Fried, Mal Freeburg, Jim La Mont, George Miles, Andy Hufford, R. Lee Smith and L. S. "Deke" DeLong.

The distinctive gold wings designed for Northwest pilots by Col. Brittin in 1929, and still worn today, are shown in reproduction of air mail stamp issued in 1930 and shown below. The U.S. Post Office Department adopted the Northwest wings for this issue. Using the same wings, a special air mail flag was dedicated by second Postmaster General Glover and accepted by the Post Office Department at the Post Office Air Mail Exhibit at Allerton House, Chicago, during the week of the National Air Races. The new flag was designed by Col. L. H. Brittin, vice president and general manager of Northwest Airways, for use in the air mail service. Postmaster General Glover pointed out that the flag should fly over every airport to designate the point on the field where air mail is dispatched. Today, some retired pilot's wings are handed down to newer captains as a symbol of continued service.

Above: On July 1, 1930, Northwest began operations from their new $100,000 terminal facilities at St. Paul's municipal airport. General offices formerly located at the Merchants Bank Building in St. Paul were moved here. Previous base of operations at Wold-Chamberlain Field, Minneapolis, was retained as an intermediate stop with expanded passenger facilities. Ford Trimotor NC 8419 shown here (Company No. 33) is being loaded for a Chicago departure.

FIRST STEWARDS

The fourteen-passenger Ford Trimotors were placed into service by Northwest in September, 1928. Chadwick B. Smith, chief pilot, flew the inaugural flight to Chicago via Milwaukee. Stewards were aboard Ford flights to sell and collect tickets, fuel the aircraft, load baggage and mail and see to passenger comfort. Shown at right is Bob Hohag, one of the first stewards. Robert Johnston, Joe Kimm and Bertrum Ritchie were the other first stewards; all but Johnston became Northwest pilots. Kimm is probably credited with the first motion sickness containers on airliners. Early in his steward career, he carried a supply of brown paper bags for such emergencies. "Trouble was," mused Kimm, "I had to rush for the 'john' before the bottoms fell out!"

25

Mal B. Freeburg, in above 1930 photo, came to Northwest as a transport pilot and licensed mechanic in December, 1928. In a Waco taper wing, a sister ship to the one in this photo (Company No. 7), Freeburg saved a train from certain destruction by dropping flares to warn the locomotive engineer of a burning railroad bridge he had spotted while flying the night mail from the Twin Cities to Chicago. Among the passengers aboard the train was U.S. golf pro Bobby Jones. Two years later, in 1932, shortly after takeoff from St. Paul in a Ford Trimotor with Joe Kimm as co-pilot, the plane suddenly jolted as an outboard propeller snapped. Freeburg fought for control as the disabled engine jerked from its mounting and lodged in the wing struts, damaging the landing gear. The 500-pound engine poised delicately as a potential bomb to whatever precariously lay below. After regaining control, the veteran pilot flew carefully over the Mississippi River, put the Ford in a steep bank and shook the engine loose, dropping harmlessly into the water below. An emergency landing was made 25 miles away and eight passengers and crew were safe and sound. Captain Freeburg was awarded the first Congressional Air Mail Medal of Honor by President Roosevelt in 1933. He also received the first Distinguished Service Medal ever presented to an airline pilot by the U.S. Junior Chamber of Commerce. Freeburg was operations officer for Northwest in 1933; in 1943 he became chief pilot and in 1949 was named operations executive. He retired in 1952 with 24 years of service with the company and died May 10, 1963 in Anaheim, California, after a long illness. His son, James M. Freeburg, has been a captain with Northwest since July, 1948, and currently flies out of Seattle, Washington.

Below: New terminal facilities at Wold-Chamberlain Field were dedicated on September 19, 1930. The former Speedway Field was named in honor of Lt. Ernest G. Wold and Lt. Cyrus Foss Chamberlain, Minneapolis flyers killed in World War I.

Hamilton NC 7791 (No. 21), left, and Ford NC 8419 (No. 33) prepare to depart Wold-Chamberlain Field's new terminal building on flights to Chicago via two routes with intermediate stops. The fare to the "windy city" was $30 one-way. Average flying time was 2 hours, 45 minutes. Northwest's original hangar appears in background over Ford. Hangars at left are of the Naval Reserve Station.

Right: Al Erickson prepares to fuel No. 33 at Holman Field, St. Paul, on its return flight from Chicago. Photo by George F. Johnsen.

27

Chapter 2 — WINGS WESTWARD

The depression that beset the United States in the early thirties challenged industry and individuals for financial survival. Paradoxically, Northwest Airways began seeking air mail routes westward in its endeavor to remain solvent by expansion. In its quest for a northern transcontinental line, air mail, passenger and express service was inaugurated from the Twin Cities to Pembina, with connections for Winnipeg, via Fargo and Grand Forks, North Dakota, on February 2, 1931. The following June, further westward progress came with service extension to Bismarck-Mandan, North Dakota via Valley City and Jamestown.

During this period of time, a series of dramatic changes took place within the company, beginning with the untimely death of operations manager Charles W. Holman as a result of a crash in his famous Laird racing plane. Chief pilot Chad B. Smith, who assumed Holman's position in May, 1931, died suddenly during an operation on September 12, 1931. Pioneer Twin Cities aviator Walter Bullock was named operations manager on October 1, 1931, coincidentally on the fifth anniversary of Northwest Airways.

In a 1933 government move to economize, air mail payments to contractors were cut back necessitating Northwest's discontinuing service to Green Bay and Madison, Wisconsin and Duluth, Minnesota, the latter having been served by Sikorsky S-38 amphibians since May 30, 1931.

Opposite: A Chippewa Indian chief from the White Earth reservation places an eagle claw necklace around the neck of Northwest Airways' pilot John F. Malone, making him a member of the tribe with the name "Silver Eagle." Malone flew the chief and a bucket of Lake Itasca, Minnesota water from St. Paul to the 1933 Chicago World Fair. The water was poured into a relief map replica of the lake. The map was a portion of the Minnesota State exhibit. Malone started flying with Northwest August 21, 1928. As a flying officer with the 109th Aero Squadron National Guard, Malone was called to active duty during 1934 Air Corps flying the mail and chose a military career following that assignment.

Without previous notice, a route extension from Bismarck-Mandan, North Dakota to Billings, Montana was granted to Northwest Airways by the outgoing national administration. On March 2, 1933, the company began service to that city with stops at Glendive and Miles City, Montana, using the six-place Hamilton monoplanes.

In September, 1933, Shreve M. Archer succeeded Richard C. Lilly as president of Northwest; Col. Brittin remained as executive vice president. Croil Hunter, who came to the company the previous year as traffic manager, was named vice president and general manager. E. I. Whyatt became the new treasurer.

Hunter, a native of Fargo, North Dakota, and graduate of Yale University, succeeded Col. Brittin as general manager after an outstanding seven-year record of progress by the founder. That same year marked the beginning of service to Dickinson, North Dakota in October and in December a survey flight was made to Seattle in a Ford Trimotor. 1933 schedules were laid out on a basis of 105-120 mph cruising speed. It became evident that faster equipment was needed for proper development of the routes. Northwest's answer arrived in February, 1934, with the delivery of three Lockheed "Orion" low-wing monoplanes designed to cruise at 206 mph.

The Orions had barely been placed into service when on February 19, 1934, Postmaster General James A. Farley, by executive order, cancelled all existing air mail contracts. The U. S. Army Air Corps, under the command of Major General Benjamin D. Foulois, was handed the task of flying the mail on skeletonized temporary routes.

Just prior to the government's action, Northwest's President Archer challenged that

Northwest Airways, Inc. would be liquidated, its 170 employees discharged and its $365,000 per year payroll brought to an end if the contracts were cancelled.

A United States Senate committee was formed to investigate all air mail contracts. Col. Brittin and his attorney, William P. MacCracken, Jr., were two of the principals held for contempt during the hearings.

The next month the conclusion of the committee suggested the contracts be reopened for bidding with commercial carriers. During this period of time, the unprepared and underbudgeted Air Corps sustained numerous crashes and several deaths during the short period of time. On April 20th, a conference of airline operators was called by Postmaster Farley and bids were opened for reinstatement of civilian air mail routes. Most of the companies had been reorganized due to circumstances prior to cancellation and certain contract requirements.

Northwest Airways, Inc. became Northwest Airlines. Inc. on April 16, 1934, and began operations as such the following May 24th. Missing from the roster of its officers was Col.

Brittin, who resigned from Northwest following charges of contempt of the Senate hearings.

In retrospect, all participants benefited from the explosive adjustment to air progress. The government recognized that the Air Corps was not a subservient budget item but an essential power lacking in modern equipment, aids to navigation and support facilities. The struggling airlines, although fostered from air mail contracts, soon emancipated themselves from full dependency on mail revenue to seek expanding passenger profits.

Northwest, after submitting aircraft designs and specifications to Lockheed Aircraft Corporation, scooped their competitors in July, 1934, with delivery of the first Lockheed "Electra" 10-A twin-engine modern airliner. With the Electras, flying time from the Twin Cities to Seattle on their new northern transcontinental route was thirteen hours of passenger comfort.

With Northwest Airlines established as an important United States air carrier, the stage was set for development of passenger service and volume.

On February 2, 1931, Northwest extended service to Pembina, North Dakota via Fargo and Grand Forks, using the Hamiltons as equipment. NC134E in above photo is being refueled for trip to the border stop.

Right: Northwest mechanics Al Lechelt (standing) and Clarence "Nippy" Opsahl (in cockpit) congratulate each other on the success of their "Iron Horse" engine test stand. The fuselage was formerly a Pheasant biplane. The powerful engines almost made the wingless bird airborne until it was chained down. On one occasion, during shift change, a propeller was mounted on the test engine but not secured. The oncoming shift test mechanic fired up the engine and the prop did a waltz down the ramp! Opsahl photo.

Above: Charles "Speed" Holman beside his Laird, taken shortly before his fatal crash. John. F. Malone photo.

Right: In 1924, Speed fitted his converted Thomas-Morse¯ with extra gas tanks, got a $500 advance from Washburn-Crosby Company, a forerunner of General Mills, and finished second in his first race from Minot, N.D. to Dayton, Ohio. Engine is an OX-5; the "Tommy" originally had a rotary engine.

Above: Mrs. Charles W. Holman, who said of her husband, "It was his whole life; he would fly anywhere, talk to anyone, if he thought it would advance aviation."

Right: Black Laird "Solution" as it appeared fully modified. Power was J-6-9 Wright engine. Large fuel tank replaced front cockpit.

"Here he come — There he goes!" That was the cry when Charles "Speed" Holman, one of the most colorful figures of early-day aviation, roared across the sky. Consider these records: 1923 — won stunt flying contest, National Pulitzer races, St. Louis. 1924 — took second place in "On to Dayton" race, Minot, N.D. to Dayton, Ohio. 1926 — hired by Northwest Airways as its first pilot. 1927 — won National Air Derby, New York to Spokane, Washington. 1928 — established world record of 1,433 consecutive loops. 1928 — won Los Angeles to Cincinnati Air Derby. 1929 — established air mail speed record for a commercial plane over an established route. 1929 — piloted the first Ford Trimotor to do an outside loop (10 times). 1929 — won 800-cubic inch closed-course race at National Air Races, Cleveland. 1930 — won $10,000 Thompson Trophy National Air Race. "Speed," who won his nickname because of his adeptness at motorcycle racing before he became a pilot, was killed stunting at an Omaha air show on May 17, 1931. The safety belt in his famed black Laird biplane "Solution" either broke or became unfastened as he flashed upside down past the grandstand. Fighting for control, Holman crashed to the horror of the crowd. His body was brought back to the Twin Cities and buried atop Pilot's Knob at Acacia Cemetery; one hundred thousand people attended the funeral. The St. Paul airport is named for Charles W. Holman. The airport marker inscription reads in part, ". . . He belonged to the heights and the heights claimed him . . ."

On May 30, 1931, Northwest inaugurated service to Duluth, Minnesota, which had no airport. The problem was solved with the purchase of two Sikorsky S-38 amphibians, a model "B" NC 303N (No. 40) shown above, and model "C" NC 199H (No. 41). The Sikorskys commuted between the Twin Cities and Duluth boat harbor at Lake Superior.

Right: Captain Jerry H. Sparboe and co-pilot John Woodhead seated in cockpit of Sikorsky S-38 during a flight to Duluth. Sparboe flew the first flight to the northern city.

Left: Camille L. (Rosie) Stein, secretary to Col. Brittin, stops for quick photo beside Sikorsky before flight to Duluth. Rosie, who was with Col. Brittin in the St. Paul Association, helped found Northwest Airways as a highly efficient "paper" handler.

33

Pilots C. L. "Les" Smith and Bill Straith take a break while Stinson Detroiter NC 2707 (No. 4) is being refueled by Walter Kollath at Madison, Wisconsin. Madison was first served by Northwest November 23, 1927. Opsahl photo taken summer, 1931.

Right: Unidentified lad and Stinson SM-2AB "Junior" NC 872 (No. 15) at Madison the summer of 1931. This ship was lost in January, 1932, when the pilot made an emergency landing in the fog after his fuel ran out. Opsahl photo.

The cover at right represents Northwest's route extension to Mandan, N.D. on June 2, 1931. The inaugural pilots were Carl F. Luethi and C. L. "Les" Smith. The route out of Fargo serviced Valley City, Jamestown, Bismarck and Mandan.

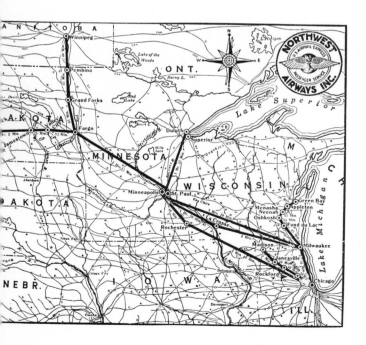

Map at left shows the Northwest route system at the end of 1931.

Chadwick (Chad) B. Smith, right, joined Northwest in July, 1927, at the urging of Charles Holman, whom he succeeded as operations manager after Holman's untimely death. Born and reared in Minneapolis, Smith entered the Army Air Service cadet training school at Kelly Field, Texas and graduated a 2nd Lt. in 1924, the second highest in his class. After flying school, he entered the University of Minnesota and in 1926 obtained his license as assistant pharmacist. The same month he came to Northwest, Smith set an altitude record of 22,017 feet in an 109th Aero Squadron Curtiss. His twin brothers, Lee and Les, soon followed Chad and became captains with Northwest. At the age of 28, Smith was suddenly stricken and died during an emergency operation September 12, 1931.

On the fifth anniversary of Northwest Airways, October 1, 1931, Walter R. Bullock was named the new operations officer to succeed Chad Smith. Born in Buffalo, N.Y., Bullock came to Minneapolis by way of Texas with his parents in 1911. The fall of 1916, he entered flying school at Newport News, Virginia, and received his wings in November at the age of 17. He obtained his F.A.I. aviator certificate No. 630, dated November 29, 1916. After several years of selling, building, repairing and rebuilding airplanes, Bullock became a pilot for Northwest September 1, 1927. He and Charles Holman were sworn in as deputy sheriffs on air law enforcement for their area in 1930.

Above: This elegant Reo bus with driver Earl Phillips was used to transport crews to and from Chicago's O'Hare Field and downtown billeting. Other Northwest drivers were Charley Crooks and John Denmon.

Left: Charles "Snakes" Bouvette, Northwest station agent at Pembina, N.D. Bouvette's duties were many and varied, including monitoring the radio.

Above: NC 8410 was the third Ford Trimotor to be delivered to Northwest. Built in June, 1929, and licensed to NWA in August, it was factory No. 5-AT-48 of the 5-AT-C series. Northwest sold their Fords in 1935. NC 8410 operated briefly with Arctic Airways, Nome, Alaska, and was sold in 1937 to Star Air Service of Anchorage, Alaska, the company founded by the author's father. The veteran Ford met its demise in 1939 when it fell through the ice at Lake Spenard, Alaska, while on skis. Borden collection.

An early-day answer for airport operations during the Twin Cities snow season was this heavily weighted roller, shown below, which packed down the snow on taxi areas and runways. The disadvantage was the belated thawing in the spring. Photo at left is Holman Field, St. Paul, the winter of 1931-32.

When Northwest inaugurated service to Billings, Montana, March 2, 1933, with the Hamilton monoplanes, the Crow Indians led by Chief Big Man were given rides to show — "If the Indians are not afraid of the white man's bird, nobody else should be." Captain Bill Straith, shown in photo above, piloted the inaugural flight to Billings; Captain F. E. Kelch piloted the Bismarck-Miles City leg. K. F. Roahen photo, Billings.

Right: Captain and Mrs. Hugh B. Rueschenberg posed for this 1933 photo with Dick Logan (in coveralls) at the Billings airport on Logan's ranch, which later bore his name. Logan was colorful, friendly and well-liked by crew members and air travelers alike as Northwest station manager. Man at left is unidentified.

NO SMOKING

RADIO

A large measure of Northwest's success has been credited to its maintenance and overhaul personnel which have been rated the highest in their field. A close association between pilots and ground crews resulted in the lowest number of breakdowns and accidents. In photo above, taken inside Northwest's St. Paul hangar, is Al Lechelt, standing behind Ford engine, and Frank Toll, masking insignia on side of Hamilton. Grease was found to solve the problem of the difficult task of masking a perfect circle on the corrigated metal of the Fords and Hamiltons. "Iron horse" engine test stand can be seen in far right corner. Northwest's radio station is at left. "No smoking" sign hanging from ceiling is still there as of this writing. Page 38 and 39 photos taken by George F. Johnsen.

At left, engine mechanic Rueben Peterson secures exhaust pipe to newly overhauled Pratt & Whitney engine on Ford. Northwest was one of the first airlines to completely equip their aircraft with the new balloon air wheels shown here.

38

Right: Engine overhaul mechanic Julius Cloeter reassembles majored engine.

Left: Aircraft sheet metal mechanics like Johnny Rosbach, left, and Paul Fenske, were becoming more in demand with the advent of all-metal airplanes. Fabric covering and woodworking skills of earlier days were still required to maintain Northwest's fleet of Wacos. Most mechanics were versatile in all skills of maintenance work.

Right: Louis E. Koerner, foreman ship department, accepts engine sign-off on Ford NC 9676 from engine department foreman Henry (Hank) C. Aune. Koerner started with Northwest August 8, 1928. NC 9676, factory No. 5-AT-42, 5-AT-B series, was originally sold to Standard Oil Co. of Indiana before purchased by Northwest.

SEATTLE
SURVEY FLIGHT

In January, 1933, Northwest Airways made its historic northern transcontinental survey flight from Chicago and the Twin Cities over the Rocky and Cascade Mountain Ranges to Seattle. Before the flight in Ford NC 9676, four members of the party (left) posed for photos. From the left: Joe Kimm, co-pilot; Hugh Rueschenberg, pilot; Amelia Earhart, "observer," and Mal Freeburg, operations department. The flight linked the upper Midwest with the Pacific Northwest. Scheduled service from Chicago to Seattle began May 26, 1934, as a route extension from Billings.

In photo at right, Croil Hunter, newly named vice president and general manager of Northwest, receives congratulations from the company's new president Shreve M. Archer (left), who succeeded Richard C. Lilly. Hunter came to the company in 1932 as traffic manager.

With the Pacific Coast finally linked with the Twin Cities, Northwest transformed from a small region carrier to one of the nation's major airlines. Plans were made to increase all schedules as soon as the northern continental route was established.

LOCKHEED ORION

The Lockheed "Orion," introduced in 1931, was the first commercial airplane to successfully feature retractable landing gear. It cruised at 205 mph and was powered by a 550 hp Pratt & Whitney Wasp engine and carried five passengers. Northwest purchased three of these aircraft, NC 13747, 13748, 13749 (Nos. 50, 51 and 52, respectively). Although the Orions were considered one of the fastest airplanes of its time, it was constructed entirely of wood and not conducive to longevity. Northwest pilots reported that the manually operated retractable gear was terrific for building right arm biceps. Various photo collections show these ships with three-bladed as well as two-blade propellers. These ships were the last Orions to be purchased from Lockheed for airline usage. Northwest used these aircraft on their Minneapolis-Seattle route, but the fleet was phased out in 1935 when the CAA prohibited the use of single-engined passenger equipment with major air carriers. Ship No. 50 eventually wound up as a fighter in the Spanish Civil War. Flown by the Spanish Republican Air Force, it was shot down and destroyed in 1937.

Above photo of all three Orions at Holman Field, St. Paul, which served for a short time between the Twin Cities and Spokane. The Hamilton Metalplanes served the new western division: Spokane-Seattle-Tacoma. The Twin Cities-Chicago route was served by the Ford Trimotors. Advertisement at right appeared in Jamestown, N.D. 1934 newspaper.

Below: The Orion featured the new split flap which was very effective for slower landing speeds. Northwest's three Orions had the first wing flaps ever installed on a Lockheed airplane.

By executive order, President Roosevelt announced that all air mail contracts would be cancelled at midnight, February 19, 1934. The senate committee investigating air mail contracts then proceeded to examine Col. L. H. Brittin, vice president of Northwest Airways, who was charged with contempt of the senate for destroying papers in the subpoenaed files of his lawyer, William P. MacCracken, Jr. Brittin steadfastly clung to his explanation that the correspondence which he destroyed was strictly personal and emphatically denied Senator Hugo Black's charges that the letters in question were relevant to Brittin's seeking the assistance of the Post Office Department to coerce the National Park Airways to sell out to Northwest. The founder of the Twin Cities airline recited the history of his struggle on behalf of a corporation controlling only four percent of the air mail contracts against huge aviation companies. On February 10th, Brittin submitted his resignation "effective immediately" to Northwest President Shreve Archer and Board Chairman Richard C. Lilly. It was accepted with extreme reluctance. Four days later, based on circumstantial evidence, Brittin was sentenced to ten days in jail for Contempt of Congress. Minnesota Senator Schall termed the senate action "a damn shame." Others stated that Brittin was a scapegoat to supermagnify the air mail contract cancellation. Brittin served his ten days as a "guest" in the home of the sheriff. A highly respected man disappeared from the Northwest Airways' scene.

Right: Numerous crashes and some fatalities resulted during the short period of time the Army Air Corps flew the air mail in February, 1934. Obsolete aircraft, lack of night flying experience and instruments were some of the contributing factors, but the largest factor was very terrible late winter and early spring snow and rain storms. The Air Corps' adversities were over-exaggerated, but resulted in government recognition of the need for budgeting a stronger air arm of the Army. In May, 1934, air mail hauling returned to the commercial carriers.

Northwest Airways, Inc. officially became Northwest Airlines, Inc. on April 16, 1934, and began operations as such May 24, 1934. Four days later, service was extended to Wenatchee, Washington, "The Apple Capital of the World." Cover below depicts inaugural flight.

The Lockheed 10-A "Electra" was introduced in 1934. Northwest was the first airline to place the new, modern airliner in service. Above photo of the prototype, NC 233Y (No. 60), was taken soon after its arrival at St. Paul. Vice president for operations Fred Whittemore ferried the aircraft from the factory. At extreme left is Hank Aune. Among the group inspecting the plane are Shreve Archer, president; Croil Hunter, vice president and general manager; and Albert H. Daggett, treasurer. During 1934 and 1935, Northwest purchased 13 10-As and one 10B at a cost of $36,000 per aircraft. Powered by two 450-hp Pratt & Whitney Wasp engines, the Electra carried 10 passengers and cruised at just under 200 mph. The cabin compartment offered the latest in passenger comfort.

LOCKHEED ELECTRA
10-A

Left: Speedboat windshield similar to the Boeing 247 offered a roomy flight deck for pilots but unforeseen problems prompted Lockheed engineers to change to conventional-faired type. Here NC 233Y and NC 14244 (No. 62) are shown before conversion by Northwest mechanics. NC 14243 (No. 61) also had a rake windshield but was lost before it was converted.

The Electras served Northwest well for many years and received praise from the majorty of pilots. Flight from Twin Cities to Seattle was reduced to 13 hours.

Above: All pilots on this board, which hung in the terminal building, flew in and out of Billings.

Above: NC 14900 (No. 67) arrives at Billings westbound to Seattle. Crew changes were made here and Billings became an important mid-route operations and later training center for Northwest.

Left: The old Morrision Place in Billings where early-day crews billeted.

46

With a backdrop of one of the new Lockheed 10-As at the St. Paul hangar, a group of Northwest "oldtimers" paused for above photo. From the left: Henry "Heinie" Walstrom, Robert E. Gilsdorf, Lockheed representative (behind), Leonard Holstad, "Big Jim" La Mont, Rosie Stein, Ron Stelzig, unidentified girl, Aggie Phillips, Bill Diehl (in uniform), Clara Wanvick, girl behind unidentified, Lou Koerner, John Vars, Tom Bamberry and Karl Larson. La Mont, promoted to superintendent of maintenance in March, 1933, started with Northwest May 28, 1928, as chief ship mechanic.

Joe Kimm, left, and Captain Forrest E. Kelch chat briefly with Northwest vice president for operations Fred Whittemore, center, prior to his test-hopping "modernized" taperwing Waco, shown below. Kimm, one of Northwest's first stewards and then a co-pilot, became a captain January 1, 1935. Whittemore assumed his position in January, 1933. One stripe on uniform sleeve for co-pilot and two stripes for captain were retained by the company for many years.

Streamlined Waco at right was used into the middle 1930's on special flights for company business and smaller air mail ports of call. Bill Hamilton collection.

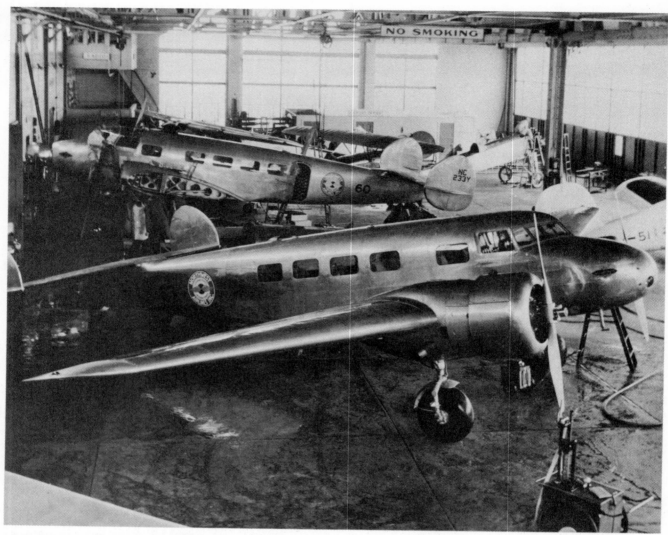

No Smoking

Four types of aircraft are shown in above photo at St. Paul hangar. Barely visible in background is a Hamilton; a Waco; the Lockheed Electra, and at right, a Lockheed Orion. Ship No. 60, the first Electra, is undergoing windshield modification during major overhaul. Northwest's home-based radio station KNWA is in upper left hand corner.

Line chief Rueben Peterson displays external power supply used in starting the Electras.

St. Paul radio operator Fred Clark, at right. Some of the early-day operators were D. W. Foote, W. J. Edwards and Lou Dunham. At the Madison station WSDR in 1931, George Benson, Alan Hall and Russell Turner twisted the dials. In 1933, the Royal Airport hangar in Madison burned down and Northwest lost all of their radio and office gear. Later, the company built a separate radio station. Pilot Clarence Bates was an early radio operator in Milwaukee and built one of the first mobile communications.

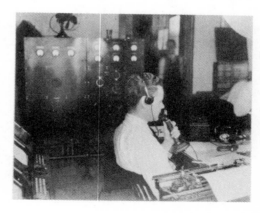

48

Upper photo taken at Fargo N.D. the winter of 1934-35 depicts typical cold-weather operations encountered on Northwest's northern continental route. Fargo radio station KNWB went on the air in 1931. Exchange of weather information, aircraft movements and passenger counts were transmitted from station to station as well as ground to air. Bates photo.

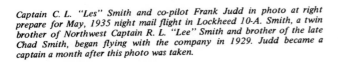

Above: Hangar at Pembina, N.D., which was the point of interchange for passengers and mail to Winnipeg, Manitoba, via Winnipeg Airways. Northwest's radio station at Pembina, KNWG, went on the air in 1931. In 1935, the Hamiltons flew directly to Winnipeg, establishing Northwest's first international service. Kimm photo.

Captain C. L. "Les" Smith and co-pilot Frank Judd in photo at right prepare for May, 1935 night mail flight in Lockheed 10-A. Smith, a twin brother of Northwest Captain R. L. "Lee" Smith and brother of the late Chad Smith, began flying with the company in 1929. Judd became a captain a month after this photo was taken.

Chapter 3 — CROIL HUNTER AND THE DC-3

Over the trail that Lewis and Clark blazed in a year and a half, on their tenth anniversary, Northwest Airlines flew modern Lockheed airliners in thirteen hours. The struggling little group of 1926 had grown into a significant air carrier.

"It required a considerable stretch of the imagination to associate a 10th birthday with the idea of maturity," general manager Croil Hunter was quoted as saying in 1936. "Yet," he continued, "in the life of transport aviation, 10 years is a ripe, old age. In fact, when you are ten, you are a hoary old pioneer!" Hunter added, "Now ... we are used to the speedy passing of ships (airliners). For as our transports roar out of terminals and streak off at three miles a minute to destinations halfway across the continent, I realize that tomorrow these ships will be supplanted with new marvels of speed, comfort and luxury."

Hunter's perception manifested itself in July, 1937, when as the newly elected president of Northwest he announced the company purchase of the new ultra-modern 260 mph Lockheed 14 "Sky Zephyr," an updated model of the highly successful Lockheed 10 "Electra." The invincible airline placed the Zephyrs on their Twin Cities-Chicago route in October, 1937, and the following January, flights were extended to Seattle.

Opposite: Croil Hunter, described by Newsweek Magazine "as casual as the snapbrim hat he wears," grasped the controls of Northwest Airlines amidst troubled equipment problems and piloted the company to new and greater heights. Photo courtesy of Mrs. Hunter.

That same month, Northwest flew into troubled skies. With almost eleven years of passenger service without a passenger fatality, the company suffered the loss of a Lockheed 14 and all of its occupants. Pioneer Pacific Northwest flyer Captain N. B. "Nick" Mamer, with co-pilot F. W. West, Jr., crashed 12 miles northeast of Bozeman, Montana. The Bureau of Air Commerce Investigating Board findings held the crash was caused by "structural failure of the upper vertical fins and rudders due to flutter which resulted in loss of control of the aircraft."

Soon after takeoff, Mamer radioed that he was experiencing tail-buffeting. Investigation of the remains of the once sleek air transport revealed that the vertical stabilizers had separated from the aircraft while in flight. The Zephyrs were temporarily grounded.

On advice of Lockheed engineers in consultation with Northwest officials, the new Lockheeds were placed back in operation with restricted power settings on the two powerful 850 hp Pratt & Whitney engines. Lockheed's contention was that excessive speed through turbulent air was a contributing factor in the Mamer crash.

Northwest suffered a second shock the following May when vice president for operations Fred Whittemore, ferrying a new Lockheed 14, NC 17394, to the Twin Cities, slammed into a canyon wall 20 miles east of Glendale, California. Lost with Whittemore were Lockheed test pilot Sidney Willey and seven others, including Northwest engineer Henry W.

Salisbury, his wife and two children. The cause of the Whittemore crash did not reflect on the Zephyr's performance, but the loss of veteran Northwest pilots Mamer and Whittemore cast a black cloud over the Lockheed 14.

Two months later on July 8, 1938, a third Lockheed 14 was lost at Billings, Montana, while attempting a takeoff with restricted power settings. Fortunately, no fatalities resulted from the crumpled wreckage.

Eventually, all the trouble-plagued airliner's empennages were modified with balance panels built into the rudders. The aircraft became completely serviceable once more.

With the full knowledge that operational bugs show up in most new aircraft, nevertheless, a group of pilots approached President Hunter and expressed their lack of confidence in the Zephyrs. Hunter pledged immediate action but asked their cooperation until such time as the equipment could be replaced; otherwise, it would cripple the company.

In late 1938, true to his word, Hunter managed to place an order for the much-in-demand new, huge 21-passenger Douglas DC-3 transport with delivery set for early 1939. In March, DC-3 service was inaugurated on the Twin Cities-Chicago route under the supervision of Northwest operations manager George E. Gardner, who succeeded Whittemore in June, 1938. A. G. Kinsman was acting general traffic manager.

With the delivery of additional DC-3s, service was extended to Seattle, Washington, April 1, 1939. Northwest's first stewardess service was added with the advent of the new airliners. The dependable Lockheed Electras flew secondary routes with 19 major stops on the system. Side tours to Glacier and Yellowstone National Parks were packaged into fares for the interested western air traveler.

Faster, more confortable equipment forecast brighter skies for Northwest Airlines with visions of further route expansions.

Northwest Airlines celebrated its tenth anniversary as a recognized United States air carrier with a bright future. The event heralded the transition from the golden years of a struggling few and many adversities to an era of new, superior leadership, modern equipment and priceless experience.

NORTHWEST AIRLINES
1926 — 1946

Lockheed 10-A Electra (No. 60) makes a brief fuel and passenger stop at Milwaukee, Wisconsin, enroute to Chicago from the Twin Cities. Doyle collection.

Below: Captain Clarence Bates, left, conducts a tour of Northwest facilities and inspection of Lockheed Electra for wealthy businessman William Ingersoll. Bates, a pioneer exhibition and racing pilot from Milwaukee, first flew for Northwest on the Fox River Valley mail run in the early 1930's. Among his many talents were photography and radio communications. He built one of the first mobile radios in the area. Bates collection.

Above: Prototype Lockheed 10-A Electra with "modernized" cockpit windows, propeller spinners and rubber deicer boots. Photo taken February 15, 1936, over Twin Cities winter scene. Photo by George Johnsen.

On July 15, 1937, former vice president and general manager Croil Hunter was named president and general manager. Hunter, a native of Fargo, N.D. and a Yale graduate, came to Northwest as traffic manager in 1932. An exceptional administrator, Hunter maintained communications with all his personnel and possessed a likeable, humble quality that captured the dedication to the company from the lowest echelons to staff people alike. Other officers of Northwest were: E. I. Whyatt, secretary-treasurer; Fred Whittemore, vice president in charge of operations; and L. B. Farrington, general traffic manager. In 1937, Northwest Airlines advertised the shortest in miles — fastest in schedules — and lowest in fares to Seattle and points west. The fare on their newly announced three round-trips daily from Chicago to Seattle was $100 one-way and $166 round-trip with only 13½ hours flying time between the two points. Hunter succeeded L. M. Leffingwell, who became president of the company in 1935.

At Pembina, N.D., a connection point served by Northwest for air travel in Canada via Winnipeg, Manitoba, this group in above 1937 photo are, from the left: Co-pilot Ray Norby; Co-pilot Clarence "Nippy" Opsahl; Captain Bill Richmond; unidentified U.S. Custom's officer; unidentified Northwest station manager, and Canadian Custom's Chief "Big Mac" Mac Martin. Richmond, a former U.S. Army Air Corps pilot, flew the air mail for the Army during the air mail contract cancellation in 1934, while under the March Field, California command of then Lt. Col. "Hap" Arnold. He began flying for Northwest May 15, 1935, with hundreds of flying hours to his credit. Opsahl collection.

Left: Twin Cities flight dispatcher Ronald Stelzig in 1937. Stelzig began his career with Northwest as a passenger agent in 1930.

Radio operator Harry Morton, in photo at right, as a member of a vital link to all Northwest stations — radio communications. Early-day communicators like Robert B. Kuehn, Jack Webb and Joseph A. Cheek joined Morton with radio traffic concerning aircraft locations, weather and manifests. Robert Bates collection.

The twin-engine Lockheed 14-H (also known as the Zephyr and Model 14) was introduced in 1937 and was larger and faster than its Lockheed predecessor, the 10-A or Electra. The 14-H introduced several new developments including the single spar all-metal wing, the Lockheed-Fowler flap and the integral wing-type fuel tank. Northwest Airlines eventually operated 11 Zephyrs beginning October 1, 1937, with inauguration flights between the Twin Cities and Chicago. The Chicago-Twin Cities-Seattle Lockheed 14-H service began January 1, 1938. Howard Hughes set a world record in 1938 when he flew a Model 14 around the world in 3 days, 19 hours and 14 minutes. Above photo is NC 17385 (No. 85), Northwest's fourth Zephyr put into operation.

LOCKHEED ZEPHYR 14-H

Below: The first Lockheed 14-H, NC 17382 (No. 82), is accepted by Northwest Airlines at Las Vegas, Nevada. As the letter "X" in the tail number denotes, Northwest received the prototype aircraft as they did with the Lockheed Electras. Famous Fowler flap track farings can be seen on trailing edge of the wing. Note the absence of rudder balance panels which became an early, major modification for the high-speed Zephyrs. Powered by twin 850 hp Pratt & Whitney Hornets, the Model 14's carried 12 passengers and a crew of two. Rated top speed was 244 mph, with cruise speed at 223 mph.

Above: Interesting, clear, close-up photo of Lockheed 14-H gives the viewer an idea of the hugeness of the new airliners. Often referred to by Lockheed as the "Super Electra," it housed the ADF loop antenna in a plexiglass nose cone that later became the bombardier station in the Hudson bomber military version of the Model 14. Below: Northwest logo which was introduced with the Zephyrs and used extensively in advertising. Doyle collection.

Above and left: With the inauguration of the Lockheed 14-H, Northwest dropped their famous fuselage emblem and changed to winged "Northwest" lettering above passenger windows. The emblem reappeared again when the company placed Douglas DC-3 aircraft in service in 1939. Photos courtesy Mrs. Croil Hunter.

Below: Croil Hunter watches as Lockheed 14 takes off from Logan Field, Billings, Montana, September 25, 1937. Photo courtesy Mrs. Croil Hunter.

Captain Nick B. Mamer, right, co-pilot Frederick W. West and eight passengers were killed January 10, 1938, in a crash of Lockheed 14-H, NC 17388. Investigation of the wreckage 12 miles northeast of Bozeman, Montana, revealed the cause of Northwest's first passenger fatalities since the company was founded was separation of the fins and rudders from the aircraft due to flutter. Mamer, a pioneer Spokane, Washington aviator, placed third in the 1927 New York-Spokane National Air Race, which was won by Charles "Speed" Holman. Prior to flying for Northwest Airlines, Mamer operated Mamer Air Transport at Felts Field, Spokane. James Borden collection.

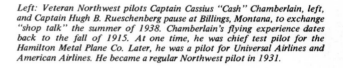

Left: Veteran Northwest pilots Captain Cassius "Cash" Chamberlain, left, and Captain Hugh B. Rueschenberg pause at Billings, Montana, to exchange "shop talk" the summer of 1938. Chamberlain's flying experience dates back to the fall of 1915. At one time, he was chief test pilot for the Hamilton Metal Plane Co. Later, he was a pilot for Universal Airlines and American Airlines. He became a regular Northwest pilot in 1931.

Right: George E. Gardner was appointed Northwest's operation manager in June, 1938. For five years Gardner was with the U.S. Bureau of Air Commerce, during which time he organized the government's airline inspection service and became its first assistant chief inspector in charge of airline regulations. In September, 1937, he was western division superintendent of Northwest, with headquarters at Spokane, Washington. In August, 1939, Gardner was promoted to vice president and director. Years later, he became president of Northeast Airlines. R. C. Anderson collection.

Above: September, 1938 photo of Northwest's maintenance personnel was taken at the St. Paul hangar. Front row, from the left: Ted Hallen, John Rossbach, Harold Kittleson, Shorty Hughes, Roy Philblad, Bill Hoffman, Ed Krueger, Charley Meyers, unidentified, John Mooney, Bud Lemenager, Cecil Iffert, Nels Larson, unidentified, Quinn, Lars Hjermstad, unidentified, Wally Anderson, M. Bissonnette, Rueben Peterson, Fred Fumder, Tiny Couninan, Chet Larson. Second row: (L-R) Leo Meyers, Reimnoldt Pinke, Ortem (Ray) Rahr, Walter Greer, Earl Karnstedt, Wally Lingby, Al Opsahl, Bill Peterson, Enricho (Bob) Martino, Hugh Bolander, Bud Winter, Paul Fenske, Bill Fraser, Harold Hodgson, Ray Pieper, Clarence Johnson, Mannace Baker, Fred Burch, Orville Tosch, Marvin Osterfeldt, Earl Pokela, Bill Misfeld, Harold Gilliland and Carl Sorleim. Back row: (L-R) Clif Ablam, Dick Howard, Wade Stanley, Manfred Boe, Joe Schuster, Shorty Heinrich, Burton Quam, Ed Mathews, Chet

Right: 1938 air photo of Wold-Chamberlain Field with paved runways and complete disappearance of old speedway concrete race track. Ken Brommers photo.

...arl Base "Northwest Airlines Inc" Sept 10th 1938.

Mahannah, Clarence Fleischman, Len Pokela, Cliff Stone, August Sombech, Ben Foster, Martin Leadon, Emil Heideck, Slim Cady, Johnson, Pete Shields, Les Johnson, Hank Aune, Sarge Richter, Lou Koerner, Norris Mickelson, Carl Magnuson, Chuck King, Bob Wagner, Ev Olson, Fred Priesmitz, Don Benson, unidentified, Lloyd Nelson, Simes, Ralph Geror and Cal Cahoon appears in window of office, above rear. Minneapolis personnel who do not appear in this photo were: Hjalmar Rosedahl,

Clarence Magnueson, Leo Holt, Patrick Lendway, Gene Roggeman, Hiram Scovel, Orville Kane, Tom Hillis, Marvin Cooney, Del Cooney, Kenneth Dorsey, William Hohag, Edward Poe, Archie Barley, Leonard Stokes and Dean Robertson. Many thanks to Norris Mickelson and Harold Hodgson for long hours spent identifying their former co-workers. Note rudder balancer cutaways on fin of Lockheed 14-H undergoing overhaul. Harold Hodgson photo.

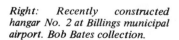

Right: Recently constructed hangar No. 2 at Billings municipal airport. Bob Bates collection.

Above and left: Captains Frank Ernst, left, and Clarence Bates inspect quick-detach Federal skis mounted on Fargo-based Hamilton. In January, 1939, the plane was flown to Minneapolis, then Milwaukee, to fly air mail and express into snowbound Chicago. Northwest Airlines was the only carrier able to operate in and out of the "windy city" before the heavy snowfall was removed from the runways. Ernst first flew as a Northwest captain in May, 1937. Bob Bates collection.

Heralding the arrival at the Twin Cities of Northwest's new Douglas DC-3 are avid cyclists Jack Hogin, left, Lloyd Belden, center, and Bud Stahel. The trio reminds the reader that the Wright Brothers built bikes before they created their famous airplanes.

DOUGLAS DC-3

The Douglas DC-3 became standard equipment on many of the world's airlines in the late 1930's. Northwest took delivery of its first truly modern 21-passenger airliner in April, 1939, at a cost of $125,000. Powered by twin 1,200 hp Pratt & Whitney engines, the designed cruise speed was 185 mph at 10,000 feet. Northwest purchased a total of ten DC-3s before WW-II commercial production was halted. First bird was NC 21711 (No. 1 and later No. 301). Above is NC 21716 (No. 6-No. 306), a Douglas DC-3 leased from American Airlines was used for crew training and Twin Cities-Chicago service in March, 1939.

Above: Flight deck and instrument panel of Douglas DC-3. Full-feathering propellers, automatic pilot and advanced radio gear and instruments were some of the features of the new airliner. Pilots liked the good cockpit visibility for both ground and air operations. Photo at right of DC-3 plush interior of 21-passenger configuration, featuring many passenger conveniences.

63

FIRST STEWARDESSES

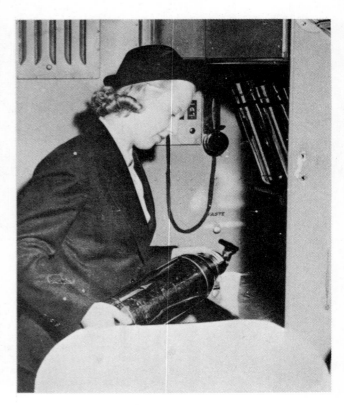

Northwest added stewardess service with the new Douglas DC-3s. Pictured above is Dorothy Stump, one of the first stewardesses hired by the Twin Cities airline. Miss Stump retired in June, 1951, having flown all the domestic and international routes operated by the company. In photo at right in Virginia "Ginny" Johnson, second stewardess to join Northwest with Dorothy Stump. Other early-day stewardesses were: Louise (Jerry) Rudquist, Jessie McLeod, Eunice Otsea, Flora Queen, Grace Lanigan, Catherine Thom, Burnece Sorby, Olga Loken and Lois Long. R. C. Anderson collection.

(L-R) Wayne Wallers, Gene Dodge, Leo Holt and Tom Hillis pose in front of DC-3, NC 21714 (No. 4), at St. Paul the summer of 1939.

Chicago to Seattle DC-3 service was operated by Northwest early in 1939. No. 2 ship is beautifully captured on film above at Felts Field, Spokane. Crews stationed here flew two routes: Seattle-Yakima-Portland and Spokane-Wenatchee-Seattle. H. T. de Mers collection.

Right: Boeing B-17 "Flying Fortresses" based at McChord Field, Washington, pass between Northwest DC-3 and Washington's majestic Mount Rainier. H. T. de Mers collection.

Left: Air mail being loaded at Boeing Field, Seattle. Side arms shown here were required to be carried by all who handled the mail. In earlier days, pilots also wore guns.

65

No — they're not from a Broadway show — they're new stewardesses of Northwest Airlines. Selected for poise and attractiveness, these nurses shown above inspected the giant Douglas DC-3 before beginning instructions for their new positions. (This is the first class conducted for the airline.) Chosen from a long list of applicants are, left to right, Alyce Grangaard, Lucille M. Fischer, Catherine Agnes Shaughnessy, Margaret "Donnie" Donovan, Beatrice M. Gilbert, Dorothy M. Baughman, Corinne Isabelle Juelson, Kathleen A. Monsebroten, Mary Jo Smith and Ardis Mae Johnson. H. T. de Mers collection.

Right: Rival of Klondike Kate for fame of the Alaska wilderness is pretty, diminutive Mary Joyce. From the far reaches of her Tauku Lodge in southeastern Alaska, Miss Joyce became a stewardess with Northwest in 1940. Among her noted accomplishments are dog team musher, radio operator, river pilot and flyer. The winter of 1935-36, the famed Alaskan mushed 1,000 miles from Tauku, B.C. to Fairbanks, Alaska. The following July, she received national publicity for being instrumental in the rescue of "Glacier Priest" Father Bernard Hubbard, whose wrecked boat marooned him on a Twin Glaciers river rock. Miss Joyce doffed the parka for a uniform of the Northwest stewardess during the summer months for several years. H. T. de Mers collection.

First known aerial stowaway, young Gordon Mullen of Renton, Washington, is shown in photo at right in "custody" of a Fargo, N.D. policeman. Startled stewardess Eunice Otsea, left, discovered Mullen in the aft blanket compartment during an April, 1940, Seattle-Billings flight. The runaway had crawled through the DC-3 baggage compartment and bedded down in the softest spot in the airplane. Fargo police fed and housed the lad until he could be returned to his home, courtesy of Northwest Airlines. Fargo station manager Dave Evans, right, inspects the unorthodox entrance. Opsahl collection.

Below: 1940 air view of Boeing Field, Seattle, looking toward Elliott Bay. The airport was built in 1928-29 and named in honor of William E. Boeing, founder of the famous Boeing Airplane Company. The gateway airfield was soon to become the second home of Northwest Airlines. At center left can be seen Boeing Plant #2, which produced many famous aircraft, including the B-17 "Flying Fortress." H. T. de Mers collection.

67

Above:. Familiar DC-3 retraction of right landing gear, then left, Northwest Douglas NC 21777 (No. 7-307), departs Boeing Field for Billings and points east. An accountable 36 DC-3s were purchased by the company in 19 years of service. H. T. de Mers collection.

Left: Northwest Seattle-based passenger agent Hart de Mers congratulates stewardess Lucille Fischer on her August, 1940 solo flight at Boeing Field. de Mers, who had been with the company several months, was glad to get his $65 per month position. The esprit de corps of all Northwest employees manifested a unified pride of association despite strict company fraternization rules. Passenger service crews flipped coins for pickup of in-flight box lunches in Seattle. The lucky toss assured an extra meal to augment their slim budget. Agents were cunning in luring passengers away from "the other outfit." H. T. de Mers collection.

Right: Brothers with Northwest, Willis (left) and Lyle H. Strong, exchange notes beside Lockheed 10-A Electra. Lyle learned to fly in his native state of Minnesota in 1929. He first flew for the company in 1935, after barnstorming in the Midwest for several years. He retired in 1968 for medical reasons and died February 24, 1972. Willis began flying for Northwest in June, 1940, and died of cancer in the early 1960's.

Seattle-based Captain D. S. (Dudley) Cox, left, and co-pilot William F. Wallace take a break during brief stop at Helena, Montana, the winter of 1940-41, in photo at right. Cox first flew as captain for Northwest in March, 1938. Wallace learned to fly at Oakland-based Boeing Flying School in 1930, after completing a master mechanic's course on his father's advice. He came to Northwest as a co-pilot in July, 1939, and checked out as a captain in late 1941. Wallace photo.

Below is shot of DC-3, NC 21715, at St. Paul.

Rochester, Minnesota hangar area, at right, signifies an important stop for Northwest since it began service to the home of the world-famous Mayo Clinic in 1930. Through the decades, Northwest has offered special services for ambulatory patients.

Chapter 4 — NORTHWEST'S MAJOR WW-II CONTRIBUTIONS

The year 1941 in the United States could be described as one of bustling economy, industrial progress and a country on the move. A deceptive peacefulness that prevailed over the land was shattered at year's end. The devastating reality all Americans dreaded happened — Pearl Harbor and World War II.

Overnight ... enlistment, rationing and priorities became daily by-words. Instant changes were triggered affecting every citizen and business. The airline industry became one of the first businesses beset by drastic changes: Army control, veteran captains called to active duty, dramatic cuts in domestic service, to name a few. Northwest Airlines schedules between the Twin Cities and Chicago were cut from seven to three trips a day, Fargo-Seattle flights were reduced to one a day, as was Fargo-Winnipeg. Spokane-Portland and Twin Cities-Duluth service was cancelled.

Early in 1942, Northwest was chosen by the U. S. Army to set up an aerial supply route to Alaska via the inside route over the Canadian prairies. It was the Army's contention that a commercial airline, accustomed to flying under winter conditions, could best develop such a route quickly and efficiently. With its base of operations established at railhead Edmonton, Canada, everything that could be loaded intact or dismantled was flown to Alaska over the Fort St. John, B. C.-Whitehorse, Y. T.-Fairbanks route with intermediate stops at Fort Nelson, B. C. and Watson Lake, Y. T. Veteran Northwest pilot Frank Judd was named superintendent of the new northern region with Dale Merrick as his assistant. Longtime employee Tom Nolan was appointed superintendent of cargo. Later, the route was extended 1,600 miles out the Aleutian chain to Adak with flights carrying mail, cargo and military personnel.

In September, 1942, Northwest established a new flight training school at Billings, Montana, with Captain Earle W. Hale as its first superintendent. Northwest captains checked out Army transport pilots in Curtiss C-46 "Commando" cargo aircraft and others. In addition, radio technicians were trained for the Army. Over 700 men were processed in all phases of large transport operations.

A huge bomber modification center was opened at Holman Field, St. Paul, where more than 5,000 employees engineered and installed special equipment, much of it secret. In excess of 3,000 aircraft destined for overseas passed through the facility. At Vandalia, Ohio, a similar center was established for modification and testing of aircraft.

Keeping pace with steadily increasing activities, Northwest enlarged its executive staff in 1942. President Hunter announced the appointment of E. I. Whyatt as vice president. Whyatt started with the company as assistant treasurer in 1932. The following year, he became treasurer and was secretary treasurer at the time of his election to the new post.

Opposite: End-of-the day, testing B-24 Liberator bombers modified at Northwest's St. Paul center are: (L-R) Captains C. L. "Les" Smith, L. J. "Jerry" Koons and Bert Ritchie. Over 3,000 bombers were test flown by Northwest pilots. Smith and Ritchie have been with the company since the 1930's. Koons first flew as captain in September, 1940.

K. R. Ferguson, a licensed pilot since 1929, came to Northwest as Minneapolis traffic manager in 1932. His new position of vice president in charge of operations filled that vacated by George E. Gardner, who was called to active duty as a colonel in the Army Air Corps. R. L. "Lee" Smith was named the new operations manager.

Another promotion was A. E. Floan to the position of secretary. Floan, a practicing St. Paul attorney prior to his appointment as Seattle-based district traffic manager, returned later to the Twin Cities to head up the airline's Bureau of Economic Research. Northwest's post-war expansion program was based in part on surveys he conducted.

That same month, Northwest Airlines had men in every branch of United States armed forces. Northwest furnished flight personnel for Army contract work assigned to the aeronautical division of the Minneapolis-Honeywell Regulator Company engaged in development and manufacture of electronic control systems for aircraft, many of which played an important role in the post-war aircraft picture.

A special project of major importance, ice research, was conducted at Twin Cities Wold-Chamberlain airport under the jurisdiction of Air Transport Command and later, the Wright Field Army experimental station. Northwest contributed mechanics, engineers and pilots to this all important segment of the war effort and post-war aviation.

Across the way from the ice research headquarters in a Navy building at Wold-Chamberlain, the Twin Cities airline contributed like personnel to project precipitation static. Extensive flights by Northwest crews were flown through moisture, dust storms and dry snow with highly successful results in solving problems of radio communications and navigation signal blockouts.

By 1944, with Allied forces determining a successful outcome of hostilities, some military cargo aircraft were released to the airlines. Conversion centers were set up commercially and by the airlines converting the aircraft for passenger service. Northwest overhaul and maintenance crews once again excelled in dismantling, scraping off olive-drab paint and refurbishing interiors; thereby transforming Douglas C-47 cargo planes into DC-3 airliners.

When the war ended in Europe, Northwest received one more military assignment. Troops had to be rushed from the East to West coast embarkation points as the tempo of attack in the Pacific was accelerated. With 14 Army transports at their disposal, the company began operating a separate airline between Newark, N.J. and Seattle, Washington, with four round-trips daily. More than 30,000 GI's had been carried at the completion of the program in 1946.

With its fleet building up and the easing of travel restrictions, President Hunter and his staff gradually phased into a post-war expansion. Pioneer day airline experience, coupled with their global involvement supporting the war effort, qualified Northwest Airlines for a bright future.

On June 1, 1945, Northwest Airlines extended its service to New York from the Twin Cities via Milwaukee and Detroit. Coast-to-coast at long last had been achieved; tomorrow, Alaska and the Orient.

Members of Northwest's skeet and trapshooting team pause for this photo at right the summer of 1941. (L-R) Hank Aune, engine shop supervisor; Harold Hodgson, maintenance; Croil Hunter, president; Marty Bissonnette, maintenance; and Joe Schuster, propeller shop. The group met at a White Bear Lake, Minnesota range once a week for two summers. Hodgson photo.

"A shot of that makes me feel like a new man!" In the Twin Cities for a study of oxygen equipment developed by Mayo Clinic scientists and Northwest Airlines' engineers, Emery M. Ellingson of Washington, D.C., right, Assistant Chief of Safety Rules and Education Committee of the Civil Aeronautics Board, tested — and endorsed — the masks used by all Northwest pilots. With Ellingson in this January, 1941 photo at right are pilot Ollie Yates and Dr. R. W. Lovelace of the Mayo Clinic, designer of the mask. Northwest was the first domestic airline to install individual outlets for oxygen connections on their aircraft.

Left: Northwest pioneered in the use of oxygen masks in high-altitude flights back in the early 1930's. In conjunction with doctors from Mayo Clinic, it began experiments that laid to the foundation of the modern airline systems. Special test flights were conducted to both coasts to determine and evaluate the reactions of air travelers.

Last of the Hamiltons, NC 537E (No. 22), was removed from service and sold in December, 1941. The veteran Model H-47 Metalplane had served the airline for thirteen years and flown on every route of Northwest. She carried three company insignias and was flown by most of the pilots of the 1920's and 1930's. Pete Bowers photo.

Douglas DC-3, NC 25609 (No. 9-309), makes a final flight before Army take-over of all U.S. airlines in early 1942. Northwest had ten DC-3s in operation at the time, with additional orders from Douglas Aircraft, when production was frozen for military cargo and transport commitments. Note "Buy War Bonds" sign in keeping with national trends since early 1940.

Northwest Airlines Twin Cities radio installation as it appeared at the onset of WW-II. Some of the wartime radio operators were: Clyde E. Hemstrom, Keith L. Bueghly, Clark A. Ward, Anthony P. Reuter, John O. Dye, Robert J. Glischinski and Patricia K. Wendtland. Carl Swanson, with Northwest since 1939 and formerly director of engineering research, was named superintendent of communications early in the war. Swanson received national recognition in 1939 when he invented a supercharged aircraft engine ignition system which was then generally used on commercial and military aircraft. Robert Kuehn photo.

The NORTHWEST AIRLINES INC. U.S. AIRMAIL BEAM

VOLUME 1   JUNE, 1942   NUMBER 1

NWA 'ALL OUT FOR WAR' BONDS

No. 1 Pledge in Bond Drive

'Ten Per Centers' Enlisting on New Front for Duration

Number one pledge in the Ten Per Cent club victory drive came from President Croil Hunter who signed in the presence of John E. Parker of Washington, D. C., left, member of the NWA board of directors, and United States Army dignitaries visiting in St. Paul.

Northwest Airlines has set out to blaze a new trail—a trail heading toward a new, mighty contribution to the nation's war effort.

Famous for its pioneering in air transportation the line now has opened a "new front" against the Axis powers with a civilian army.

On this front steady jobs are weapons. And regular incomes are ammunition.

And as volunteers step forward for mobilization they are inspired by one common thought—the grim determination to protect and preserve the American way of life.

The unique offensive which is attracting wide attention took form in the organization of a Ten Per Cent club to stimulate sale of war bonds.

Commander-in-chief of the war bond campaign is President Croil Hunter who founded the club after receiving an appeal from Secretary of the Treasury, Henry Morgenthau.

Eligible for membership in the club are NWA employes who pledge at least ten per cent of their earnings for the purchase of United States War bonds.

DRIVE SPEEDED

The club has adopted a slogan, "Pledge 10 Per Cent for 100 Per Cent Victory," and special posters have been distributed by campaign leaders.

In announcing the opening of the new front, President Hunter reviewed developments of recent months and urged all employes to support the war bond sale.

"It is," he said, "the patriotic duty of all American citizens to do what they can to hasten the victory of the United Nations in the present crisis.

"One of the best ways in which working people with regular incomes can help is by pledging their financial support for this great undertaking.

EVERYONE'S WAR

"Our government, through the Treasury department, has asked all citizens to pledge at least ten per cent of their incomes for the purchase of war bonds.

"The need for buying bonds should be obvious to every person. This is everyone's war, a war we intend to win. I know the government can count on us in this emergency."

The idea for the club was developed fast.

It came to President Hunter after he had read Secretary Morgenthau's letter regarding the needs for funds to carry to a successful conclusion the war effort.

12 BILLION GOAL

Mr. Morgenthau explained that the government had set as a goal for the 12 months beginning July 1, the sale of bonds, series E, F and G, having an initial cost value of $12,000,000,000.

"This," Mr. Morgenthau wrote, "will be equal to slightly more than 10 per cent of our estimated national income during this period.

"Working together, management and employes cannot only insure the success of this most important war effort but can lay the foundation for a program which will pay great dividends later."

The signal to open the "new front" started action in several
(Continued on Page 2)

Northwest Airlines Men in Every Branch of America's Armed Forces

On many far-flung battlefronts around the world, men from the ranks of Northwest Airlines today are fighting the war for freedom.

They are in the uniforms of every branch of the armed forces, have gone on active duty from every department in the company.

Some of the boys were reserve officers and they have been in active service since last year and many others have rallied to the colors in recent months.

Some are at the controls of planes winging toward distant shores, over strange lands, speeding to strategic bases with men and materials needed to crush the Axis.

Others are with ground forces —or at sea.

And quite a few still are in training.

All of the men who have gone into the service are using their experience with Northwest Airlines to the best advantage possible and playing important roles in the air program.

Specific information on the pilots who have joined the colors cannot be given because of military secrecy but it can be said that some are in other lands.

A movement is now under way to begin a roll of honor for the men in the service and first announcements on this will be made soon.

Suggestions have also been made to make all men in the service honor members of the NWA Ten Per Cent club.

From their various posts and duties, the NWA boys are sending regularly messages and letters to their friends who are carrying on at the home front.

Special activities among the civilian "army" recruits include everything from duties as air raid wardens and Red Cross workers to civilian defense assignments and special work.

Many of the stewardesses have been doing Red Cross work and knitting, as have wives of pilots and other employes in the company.

First issue (June, 1942) of "The Beam," Northwest's company publication. The product of the Hunter era was launched by first editor Joseph A. Ferris. "The Beam" was credited for stimulating excellent relations among all company employees by keeping them posted of events throughout the entire system of stations and personnel. Copy courtesy of Vince Doyle.

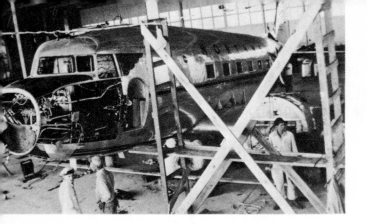

CITY OF BISMARCK

DC-3 No. 1 becomes a beehive of activity as crews prepare to remove damaged wing center section. Skin damaged by propeller has been removed from side of flight deck. Note commercial Christmas wiring strung on cribbing. Harold Hodgson photo. Below: Side view shows extensive scaffolding needed for $85,000 rebuilding of NC 21711.

Douglas DC-3, NC 21711 (No. 1), was damaged in a landing mishap at Bismarck, N.D. in August, 1942, when it hit a rough spot in the runway during its landing roll in a rainstorm. The aircraft swerved and collapsed its landing gear, causing the only injury aboard when the left propeller sliced into the flight deck injuring the veteran captain's left leg. Because of wartime conditions and the unavailability of a replacement aircraft, Northwest sent a repair crew headed by Louis E. Koerner, superintendent of aircraft overhaul, to Bismarck to rebuild the wounded bird. The major repairs, including the unprecedented change of the wing center section, were assisted by Douglas Aircraft personnel. Upon their arrival at the Bismarck airport, Koerner and his men were faced with a multitude of problems; no derrick or crane, no lights in the small-plane hangar and no scaffolding. It took the chassis of a vintage truck, parts of a rock crusher and gravel pit loading machine to solve the first problem. A pilot's observance of Bismarck on a night flight during the Christmas season sparked the answer to illuminating the hangar as strings of commercial Yuletide lights emerged from merchant's storage and were quickly strung around "Old No. 1." The entire ship was dismantled. The girders of the hangar were braced with local lumber and the fuselage was lifted. The damaged center section was moved forward and the new one, shipped from the Douglas factory, was pushed into place. Day and night the crews worked, sparked by Koerner and encouraged by their own progress. The entire passenger cabin was renovated and refinished by specialists while crews worked on the engines. The hydraulic system, radio, instruments and all controls were rejuvenated and closely inspected. By the middle of October, the job had been completed; all the crews sighed with satisfaction that the task had been finished ahead of schedule. Those with Koerner who had produced the shiny rebuilt airliner were: John Rosbach, Ken Larson, Wally Lingen, Bob Knutson, Harold Hodgson, Al Volk, Jack Deveny, and others. Festivities for the test-hop by chief pilot Don King included christening the plane the "City of Bismarck." In attendance were Governor John Moses of North Dakota, Mayor N. O. Churchill of Bismarck and other dignitaries. After his test flight, Captain King reported, "Perfect — not a single write-up."

Below: Northwest crew headed by Lou Koerner, right, stand with pride as chief pilot and captain Don King (in cockpit) prepares to test fly the "City of Bismarck." John R. Deveny photo.

Hangar, right, at Edmonton, Alberta, was the first operations headquarters for Northwest's northern division early in 1942. Later, barracks and cargo facilities were built. Tom Nolan, new superintendent of cargo under division manager Frank Judd, was put aboard an Army C-47 at St. Paul with 45 minutes notice. Sealed orders opened in flight routed them to their new headquarters via Minot, N.D. and Regina, Saskatchewan. The vital importance of their aerial supply to Alaska and the Aleutian Islands reflected in the successful removal of the Japanese occupation of Kiska and Attu Island of the Aleutian chain. Bill Cameron collection.

Aircraft engine being loaded aboard Army C-47, at left, represents the many and varied types of cargo handled by Nolan and his crews. Some other types of cargo were runway steel matting, ammunition, aircraft fuel tanks, heavy-duty road building equipment, trucks and 55,000-gallon fuel storage tanks. Outsized cargo was either partially dismantled or cut to size. Early in World War II, when fire destroyed the hospital at Nome, the government turned to Northwest and a complete 24-bed hospital, from hypodermic needles to X-ray machines, was flown in two planes from St. Louis to Nome.

At right is group of northern division Army Transport Command pilots from Northwest. (L-R) Kneeling: Lloyd Milner, Art Hoffman, Don Jones, Bob Sparkman (holding Jones' daughter), Charley Ryan (behind), Dick O'Neill, Gene Schroeder, Gil Hartley and George Montgomery. Other pilots who flew in Alaska and the Aleutians were Larry Abbey, Hal Barnes, B. S. Cooper, Jack Hazen, Earle "Cowboy" Hale, John Hart, Frank Judd, Don King, Ed La Parle, Vern Nyman, Joe Ohrbeck, Bob Olson, Clarence "Nippy" Opsahl, E. N. "Pinky" Paselk, W. E. "Red" Slaughter, Russ Sorkness, Bud Stahel, Lyle Strong, Willis Strong, Mel Swanson, Fred Zimmerly, Ray Dyjak, Frank Christian, V. A. Doyle, plus many others.

77

Left: As a test pilot on special projects for Minneapolis-Honeywell Regulator Company, Northwest Captain Clarence "Nippy" Opsahl and co-pilot Marshall H. Alworth III, prepare to fly Boeing B17 bomber aloft to compute data on several electronic devices, some highly classified, that assisted Allied bomber and fighter pilots to better reach their targets and return. One of the many improvements resulting from this program was the electronic setting of turbo superchargers aiding Army pilots to fly more precise formation. Opsahl photo.

Below: "Proud Pop" — the smiles tell the story of this big moment in the lives of these two Northwest pilots. Captain Joe E. Ohrbeck and his son, First Officer Richard S. Ohrbeck, on the first trip Pop and Son flew together as a team in July, 1943. This was the first father-son combination on airlines of the nation.

Air mail display board showing route system and Northwest's air mail statistics.

78

In June, 1942, a number of Northwest pilots check out in the new Curtiss C-46 "Commando." Chief pilot Don King and Captain Lloyd Belden had charge of many of the check flights. Northwest pilots then trained hundreds of Army Air Corps crew members at the airline's Billings training center.

Above: In front of C-46 Commando at Whitehorse, Y.T. in April, 1943, are (L-R) Lt. Chester Franecke; Captain Roman Justiss, pilot; Tom Nolan, superintendent of cargo; John Redus, radio operation, H. R. Weissenburger; Jessie Justiss, Roman's brother and co-pilot; Lt. C. E. Coffey; Bob Martino; and Todd Wright. All were members of the Army Transport Command, Alaska Wing. Harry McKee collection.

Above: Northwest Captain Bill Wallace and crew members at Fort St. John. One of Wallace's early Army cargo flights was a load of lumber. His disgust with the low priority war contribution changed when he landed at his destination, which had been out of fuel for their stoves for days. Wallace photo.

Poker — a favorite pastime between flights in and out of Adak Island in the Aleutians — is the name of the game in photo at right. Northwest pilots are Roman Justiss, left, Les McQuain, Al Henderson and Gordon Bartsch. Henderson's grin cost Justiss ten bucks to see a buried third ace. Justiss and Lloyd A. Milner were awarded the Army's Air Medal, rarely given to civilians. Frank J. Christian and Raymond J. Dyjak, killed in a December, 1944 Aleutian plane crash, received the award posthumously. Hilsen photo.

ST. PAUL MODIFICATION CENTER

A bomber modification center was opened at Holman Field, St. Paul, early in WWII. More than 5,000 employees engineered and installed special equipment, much of it secret, on more than 3,000 North American B-25 and Consolidated B-24 bombers. At Vandalia, Ohio, another such center was set up, devoted to modification and testing of aircraft. Before the war's end, with all its operations at a peak, Northwest Airlines's personnel increased from 881 to more than 10,000. Brig. Gen. E. M. Powers, Deputy Asst. Chief of Air Staff, Materiel and Services, commended Northwest for consistently meeting schedules.

Above: Barrel of 50-caliber machine gun of B-24 Sperry ball turret receives a rigid inspection. Left: Engine modifications crew test-runs B-24 Pratt & Whitney engine. Another much-needed bomber is ready for service in Europe or the Pacific.

Northwest Captain J. E. (Joe) Kimm, left, was called to active duty in the Army Air Corps in 1942. Kimm and Captain W. F. (Bill) Richmond were assigned to the Brass Hat Squadron at Washington, D.C. The pair flew special missions for high government and military officials to all points of the globe. Kimm, as a steward for Northwest Airways shortly after it was founded, soon decided the pilot had a better job and learned to fly with Chad Smith in 1931. He became a captain January, 1935, and later joined the Army Air Corps Reserve. Richmond graduated as a second lieutenant pilot from the 1932 class of the Army's Randolph Field, Texas, flying school. In 1934, he flew the air mail for the Army during the air mail contract cancellation. In 1935, he traded a military flying career for one with Northwest Airlines. He retired October 17, 1969, 40 years to the day after his first flight. Kimm and Richmond returned to Northwest after more than three years flying olive-drab airliners. Kimm photo.

A special project, ice research, was carried out by Northwest (1942-47) to circumvent crippling icing conditions on military aircraft. Originally under ATC jurisdiction and later, Wright Field, the Wold-Chamberlain-based operation involved over 110 personnel at peak activity. Below are a few of the "guys at the ice house." (L-R) Back row: Beulow, Hamlin, Butler, Hatermer, Rider. Front row: Schiebe, Gardner. "Flamin Maimie" is a North American B-25 "Mitchell" medium bomber. Veteran Northwest pilot Walter Bullock, assigned to ice research, flew every aircraft the Army had, except one or two. Tests were made in all kinds of adverse weather to combat the dread of all pilots — ice.

As WW-II Allied victory appeared in sight, a few Army transports were made available to airlines. On April 8, 1944, a multi-missioned Army C-53, originally manufactured as a DC-3A in January, 1942, arrived at Northwest's Minneapolis overhaul center and 30 days later, on May 10th, a bright and shiny DC-3, NC 33325 (No. 325), was ceremoniously presented to President Hunter "...with wholehearted cooperation and skill... in a state of completeness and perfection." The sturdy Douglas was denuded of "war paint" and completely dismantled. Step by step, the aluminum skeleton was rebuilt with enviable precision craftmanship, incorporating the latest modifications and newest systems. The ship was flown following the presentation ceremonies and pronounced the pride of the fleet by the test-flight crew.

Above: in process of "pulling an engine" are Wright Radcliff, behind propeller; Lloyd Flatten, in front on lower step; and Roy Franta, on upper step. Note the missions tallied on fuselage above engine.

Right: Unidentified employees reskinning sections of fuselage.

Below: Croil Hunter proudly accepts NC 33325 from dedicated employees. Photo courtesy of Mrs. Croil Hunter.

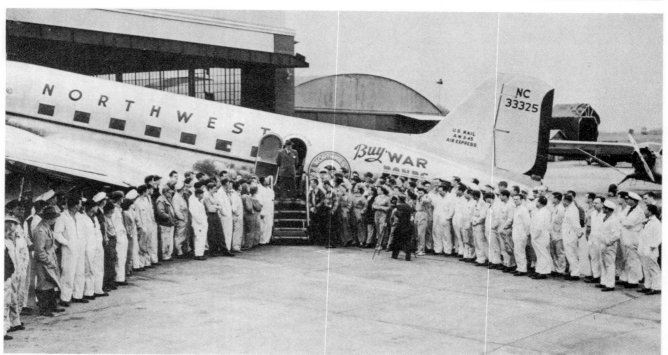

Seven Northwest DC-3s of the airline's expanding fleet appear in above late 1944 photo taken on the terminal ramp at Wold-Chamberlain Field. In preparation for the post-war era, the "family airline" converted several Army transports to commercial versions and in May, 1944, flew the first in-flight hot meals on a trip for the press from the Twin Cities to Chicago. John Deveny photo.

The Portland, Oregon airport, an important Northwest stop, was inundated by flood waters of the mighty Columbia River in early 1944. The company station temporarily relocated at Troutdale Field until reopening in August, 1944, shown at right and below.

Photo at right is Northwest Minneapolis-based service crew in April, 1945. (L-R) Hilsabeck, Lyson, O'Connell, Exbesger, Cook, Silist, Dave Pelarski, "Eager Beaver" Graham and William (Bill) Cameron. Chief mechanic was E. R. Mathews.

Captain A. J. (Bud) Stahel, left, swaps his ATC uniform for Northwest's, as many company pilots began returning to the airline. Stahel flew many missions to Alaska and the Aleutians, gaining valuable experience flying the "worst weather in the world."

Below: Last B-24 rolls out of the St. Paul modification center. Personnel shown represent a portion of the 5,000 peak-time employment. From the beginning of this Northwest operation until the final modification the day after Japan's surrender, a total of 3,286 aircraft were equipped with radar and other accouterments. A star, signifying continued production excellence, was awarded to the company during the last year for display with the Army-Navy "E" previously received.

COAST
TO
COAST

Northwest's bid for a route to New York, originally presented in 1938, was open and granted. Service was inaugurated June 1, 1945, via Milwaukee and Detroit, making Northwest Airlines one of four coast-to-coast domestic carriers. At right, Captain C. S. (Curt) Davis (on loading stand), stewardess Louise (Jerry) Rudquist and co-pilot Jerry Kilian pause for press photos before flight. The following November, service was resumed to Duluth. NC 25609 (No. 309), shown above, proudly displays coast-to-coast sign.

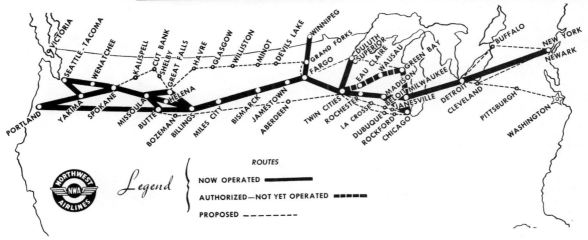

ROUTES

Legend

NOW OPERATED ━━━━━

AUTHORIZED—NOT YET OPERATED ▬▬▬▬

PROPOSED ━ ━ ━ ━

Chapter 5 — TWENTY YEARS OF PROGRESS

With world peace restored and reconstruction and rehabilitation of devastated areas commenced, feverish activity abounded in America; returning veterans, lifting of priorities, conversion of industry from military to commercial needs, and a country on the move.

Northwest Airlines, on the threshold of a gigantic expansion, set about restoring and increasing domestic schedules and repositioning their personnel. In January, 1946, the company had 388 pilots, with some still in the Armed Forces. The acquisition of the four-engine Douglas DC-4 airliners, with a four-year war proven record, dovetailed with the increased pilot numbers. Simultaneously, Northwest placed an order with the Boeing Airplane Company for ten double-deck Model 377 Stratocruisers, an airline counterpart of the military C-97. By mid-1946, an additional order for 40 twin-engined, fast Martin 202s was contracted to replace the aging Douglas DC-3s. However, only 25 of the ships were delivered to Northwest.

Based on its outstanding wartime record in Alaska and the Aleutians, Northwest Airlines had taken its place among world leaders in commercial aviation and was awarded routes to Alaska and the Orient, adding more than 12,000 miles to the system. This was of major significance, not only to the company but to the territories which it served; bringing to parts of western Canada, to Alaska and remote expanses of the Pacific, an air service of modern aircraft as a vehicle for the rehabilitation of those who were impoverished and the lands devastated by war. Alaska service to Anchorage began in September, 1946, via Seattle non-stop; Twin Cities-Edmonton January 1, 1947.

By October 1, 1946, the airline's 20th anniversary, Northwest Airlines was logged in the annuals of modern aviation as a significant leader. Company officials at that time were Croil

Hunter, president and general manager; William Stern, special assistant and member of the board of directors; Linus C. Glotzbach, vice president and assistant to the president; E. I. Whyatt, executive vice president; A. E. Floan, vice president, secretary and general counsel; W. Fiske Marshall, K. R. Ferguson and R. O. Bullwinkel, vice presidents; L. S. Holstad, treasurer; J. H. Ferris, publicity department; F. C. Judd, western region vice president; R. L. Smith, eastern region vice president; and D. L. King, manager.

Based on a July, 1946 approval by then President Truman of a certificate issued by the Civil Aeronautics Board granting routes to Edmonton, Canada; Anchorage, Alaska; Tokyo; Seoul, Korea; points in Manchuria and eastern China; Shanghai; and Manila, service was begun July 15, 1947.

By the fall of 1947, huge hangar and office facilities were constructed at Seattle's new Bow Lake Airport situated mid-way between the Queen City and Tacoma. The $1,350,000 installation was the first construction on the large field. It served as an important operations headquarters for the United States end of the Orient region. Later, air cargo, an expanding segment of commercial aviation, was extended on the Alaska-Orient route.

The Martin 202, teamed with the Douglas DC-4, was placed in service in November, 1947. This 245 mph ship, designed for fast, limited-range flights, served all the stops from the Atlantic seaboard to Billings, Montana. The DC-4 operated on the Alaska-Orient run and the soon to be phased out DC-3s operated the Billings-Spokane-Seattle-Portland routes.

The addition of new equipment and new routes prompted a change in Northwest's aircraft image. Early in 1948, the emblem that was used for over 20 years was changed to an arrow on a circular field, pointing to a northwest compass heading. The famous red tail, still used today, came into being and a wide blue stripe adorned the length of the fuselage.

Two additional, important routes were granted to Northwest. The first was awarded in

Opposite: Total eclipse of the sun, captured on film by commercial photographer Earl Chambers at the Twin Cities, graphically signifies the dawn of a new era in 1946 for Northwest Airlines, after two decades of progressive operations.

October, 1947, to Washington, D.C. via Cleveland and Pittsburgh; scheduled service commenced March 15, 1948. The second, Seattle-Tacoma-Portland-Hawaii, caused much political haggling even up to high levels, but was finally approved and Northwest inaugurated service to the Hawaiian Islands in December, 1948.

The new routes pressured Northwest for equipment. The delivery of the Boeing Stratocruisers, delayed over two years, had seriously affected the company's competitive position. In July, 1949, commensurate with the new Seattle-Tacoma airport dedication (formerly Bow Lake Airport), the huge Boeings were placed into service. By 1950, the $15 million fleet of Stratocruisers were in complete operation coast-to-coast, Hawaii and Alaska.

The know-how of Northwest Airlines was recognized in a striking manner when, at the outbreak of the Korean War, the company was assigned a major role in airlift from the United States to Tokyo, and other points of the Orient. On the basis of experience gained during WW-II, and further experience acquired in commercial service to the Orient, Northwest was named a prime contractor in this military air transport service. DC-4s previously operated by the company, and DC-4s of a number of other sub-contracting airlines, were flown and maintained by Northwest crews.

In addition to the airlift assignment, Northwest operated a special service for the United Nations involving flights between Tokyo and points of Korea. This service used DC-3 aircraft owned by the United Nations and operated exclusively by Northwest Airlines' employees. In 1950, Northwest began serving Formosa on its route between Tokyo and Manila. Back home in the Twin Cities, a $1,150,000 three-hangar line maintenance base was constructed at Wold-Chamberlain Field.

On the eve of its quarter century of operation, Northwest Airlines, Inc., now known publicly as Northwest Orient Airlines, continued its development as one of the world's major air transportation systems and placed emphasis on faster, more convenient and comfortable services for its passengers.

Below: The prototype Boeing Model 377 "Stratocruiser" test-flys over the Seattle skyline and Elliott Bay. The double-deck airliner was a counterpart of the military C-97 transport and was the first commercial Boeing produced since the 314 Clipper. The big Boeings were long range and unparalleled in passenger comfort. Boeing photo.

DOUGLAS DC-4

The Douglas DC-4, developed during WW-II as a long distance troop and cargo carrier, was the first four-engine commercial transport to be put into service by many of the world's airlines. Its military counterpart was the C-54 flown by many Northwest pilots on military leave of absence. Designed to carry 50 first-class and 62 tourist-class passengers, the big Douglas was powered by four 1,450 hp Pratt & Whitney engines, carried a crew of four or five and was designed to cruise at 225 mph at 8,000 feet. Northwest received its first DC-4 in March, 1946. Above is NX 34538 (No. 401), the second Douglas giant delivered to the company. Below is NC 6403 (No. 403).

Left: Rosie Stein, right, proudly displays the new stewardess wings just awarded to four graduates of Zell McConnel's School at Minneapolis. (L-R) Barbara Sparling, Silvia Nelson, Florence Halverson and Mary Keenan. The girls completed the three-month course in April, 1946, and received early assignments on Northwest flights.

Signing of a $15,000,000 contract for purchase of ten Stratocruisers in March, 1946, climaxes months of negotiations between Northwest and the Boeing Airplane Company, manufacturers of the luxury airliners. In photo at right are (L-R) Croil Hunter, K. R. Ferguson, vice president engineering and planning, W. E. Beall, vice president of sales, Boeing Co., and R. O. Bullwinkel, vice president of traffic, Northwest. The big airliners were not delivered until over three years later at a total cost of $20,000,000.

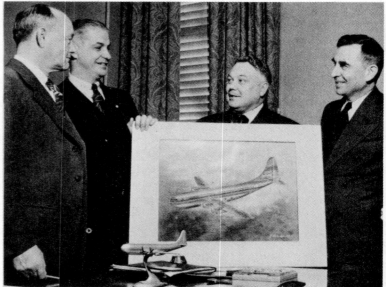

Purchase by Northwest of 40 exhaust jet-aided, five mile-a-minute luxury airliners, designated the Martin 303 (later changed to 202) at a cost in excess of $10,000,000, was announced by President Hunter in June, 1946. Photo at left is the prototype demonstrating single-engine operation. Ship was later modified — larger dorsal fin — increased wing dihedral to improve stability.

Old friends meet in above photo. (L-R) Edward V. Davis, president, Anchorage Chamber of Commerce; T. W. (Ware) Cummings, Northwest director of flight regulations; A. J. Koenig, city manager, Anchorage; Ralph Nelson; A. T. (Art) Petersen, superintendent of stations; Dudley Cox, chief pilot western region; Sid Schultz; "Chet" Brown, assistant superintendent of maintenance; Frank Judd, vice president and general manager, western region; Bob Reeve, early-day Alaskan bush pilot and president of Reeve Aleutian Airways; John F. Woodhead, operations manager.

ALASKA SURVEY FLIGHT

A mid-August, 1946 Anchorage Times newspaper ran a story with an eight column banner line, "NWA OFFICIALS HERE TO SET UP SCHEDULE." As a result of recent authorized Northwest routes to Alaska, DC-3 NC 28679 touched down at Elmendorf Field, Alaska, after a ten hour flight from Seattle. The live-wire frontier Alaskan city welcomed the return of Northwest Airlines with open arms. Special limousines were provided to carry the party the four miles between the Army field at Fort Richardson and the city proper. A typical Alaskan party featured, among other things, canned smoked salmon. On Sunday, sightseeing tours were conducted and Monday, CAA officials held day-long conferences with Northwest people. Technicalities that must be met were discussed, assuring the earliest scheduled flights up the coast would commence. While in Anchorage, Northwest arranged for hangar and ticket office space.

Above: Entertained royally at Anchorage were crew members (L-R) Sue Phelps, Marilyn Spielberger, Captain Bob Ashman and co-pilot Lloyd Rickman. Photo by H. Francis Jackson.

Camille L. (Rosie) Stein announced her resignation from Northwest Airlines August 23, 1946, for health reasons. Beloved by all the company, she was ranked as one of the oldest airline employees relating to service in the United States. Miss Stein was secretary to Col. Brittin at the time he founded the company. When Croil Hunter became president, she was his secretary. Additionally, she served as director of stewardesses 1940-41 and 1944 until she retired. Her resignation was effective October 1, 1946, giving her 20 years of service.

Northwest's Spokane station moved from its original home at Felts Field to a new $50,000 terminal at Geiger Army Field in early August, 1946, (photo right). Negotiations for land and facilities had been conducted for months. Geiger Field's larger runways could better handle the DC-4 flights and was located closer to the Spokane loop, Station Manager Lynn Schuck stated. The new station also incorporated larger hangar space and ample parking.

The Far East route and other important matters came in for discussion when directors of Northwest held their August, 1946, meeting in Seattle. Boarding the plane at Minneapolis-St. Paul are (L-R) W. F. Marshall, vice president of operations; L. M. Leffingwell, William Tudor Gardiner, Joseph T. Johnson, and Phillip D. Armour, directors; President Hunter; Edwin White and William Stern, directors. Photo courtesy Mrs. Croil Hunter.

Above: Anchorage city officials and dignitaries greeted Northwest's first scheduled flight to Alaska as passengers deplaned at Elmendorf Army Air Field near the city. A large gold key to the city was presented to President Hunter and many Pacific Northwest mayors. Captain Earle Hale skippered the flight northbound and Captain Bob Ashman commanded the southbound trip.

FIRST ALASKA
SERVICE

Below: Space for Northwest's operations in this Elmendorf Field terminal building was arranged by Frank Judd, vice president, western region. Part of the agreement with the Army resulted in Northwest installing a 24-hour eating facility.

Douglas DC-4, NC 6404 (No. 404), carrying a group of company officials headed by President Hunter, representatives of Pacific Northwest cities and regular passengers, left Seattle-Tacoma Sunday, September 1, 1946, to inaugurate Northwest Airlines service to Alaska by the "outside route." The flight arrived at Anchorage seven and one-half hours later. Among those aboard were: Mayor William F. Devin of Seattle; Mayor E. Riley of Portland; Mayor Fletcher Bowron of Los Angeles; Mayor C. B. Fawcett of Tacoma; Mayor J. V. Rogers of Wenatchee; E. H. Braden, Spokane Chamber of Commerce; T. A. Stevenson, Tacoma Chamber of Commerce; G. C. Baer, Yakima Chamber of Commerce. Start of the service culminated Northwest Airlines long bid for routes to Alaska, and returns the airline back to the Far North, where it flew extensively for the Army during the war. As this service began by the "outside route," President Hunter said service on the "inside route" from Chicago and New York through the Twin Cities gateway to Edmonton, Canada, and thence to Anchorage, probably will start in 60 days. Plans are also being made for the start of Orient flights later. After a warm Alaska reception, the inaugural flight returned to Seattle-Tacoma, arriving late that evening.

Left: Captain C. H. "Dick" Allen chats briefly with former world heavyweight boxing champion Jack Dempsey at New York. Dempsey made a December, 1946 flight with Allen to the Twin Cities where the champ refereed a boxing match. Allen learned to fly in 1930 in southern California skies and earned his commercial rating in 1931. In 1935, he graduated from Boeing Flying School, Oakland, California, and in April, 1938, he came with Northwest. In 1943, he was chief pilot of Northwest's Billings training center. Since 1952, he has been flying out of Seattle-Tacoma. As of this writing (July, 1972), Allen, who has been skippering 747s for over a year, made his last flight for Northwest without knowing it. A Northwest Airlines' pilot strike carried through his 60th birthday.

Right: A. B. "Cot" Hayes, Northwest's Alaska region traffic manager, left, greets Mr. and Mrs. Bradford Washburn on their April, 1947 arrival at Anchorage. Washburn, famous New England scientist and pioneer Alaskan mountain climber, headed up a party including RKO cameramen William Deek and George Wellestead (L-R behind Washburn) and University of Chicago physicist H. T. Victoreen (above Hayes). Others in the party were C. Robert Lange, Norman Bright, George Browne, James E. Gale and William D. Hackett. 3,000 pounds of equipment and supplies were flown in by Northwest for "Operation White Tower," the filming of the group's scientific climb of majestic Mount McKinley. Hayes, a pioneer of early-day southeastern Alaska airway operations, was chosen by Northwest to head up their Alaska station in 1946. Hayes photo.

Mr. and Mrs. Croil Hunter deplane at Tokyo, completing a survey flight to the Orient via the great circle route. Original survey flight, April, 1947, in a DC-3 (NC 33325), was piloted by Captain Ralph Nelson with Don King, Orient region manager; Frank Hass, navigator; Stanley Carlson, radio. The history-making airport inspection trip was made possible by the installation of six 100-gallon fuel tanks in the cabin compartment. AP photo, Tokyo Bureau, Japan.

FIRST ORIENT SERVICE

After nearly a year of preparation, on July 15, 1947, Northwest Airlines inaugurated its new regular route to the Orient, an event significant both to aviation and the progress of the Twin Cities airline. The new route emphasizes the lesson which the history of transportation has taught: That with each development, as distance is erased, the world, in effect, shrinks. The time from the Twin Cities to Tokyo was now only 33 hours. The first schedules were on a thrice-weekly basis. Ceremonies were conducted at New York, Twin Cities and Seattle.

Crew members of the first flight leaving the Twin Cities for the Orient were, bottom to top: Jerry Koerner, flight radio operator: Donald Rector, flight mechanic; George T. Bickel, navigator; Virgil R. Carlson, purser; Larry M. Horner, first officer; Evelyn Currie, stewardess; Ed La Parle, captain.

Above: President Hunter officiated at ceremonies after platform and crowd moved from original Wold-Chamberlain site to a Northwest hangar, prompted by a rainstorm. Dean J. Hanscom, western traffic manager, conducted ceremonies at Seattle. Crew members on the northern leg of the route were: Captain Bob Polhamus, Captain Jerry Brower, stewardess Jean Overland and Lou Everts.

Left: Barbara Wallen, Northwest Airlines Aquatennial queen dressed in Chinese costume, gives scrolls to Captain Ed La Parle to be presented to General Mac Arthur, Mayor K. C. Wu of Shanghai and President Manuel Roxas of the Philippine Republic. At right is Franklin Armstrong, master of ceremonies.

Right: R. L. "Lee" Smith, vice president in charge of eastern region, speaks as representative of Northwest Airlines at La Guardia Field, New York ceremonies. Universal News Reel and NBC Television covered the christening of Northwest's DC-4 "Shanghai." Captain Joe Kimm then flew the plane on the eastern leg.

Twenty years of passenger service is depicted in photo at left. Byron G. Webster of Chicago, first passenger carried by Northwest Airlines in July 1927, shows string of air travel tickets to stewardess Louise (Jerry) Rudquist. Original ticket in his left hand was presented to President Hunter commemorating the event.

As a part of Northwest's rigid maintenance program, aircraft are periodically dismantled at major repair depots. All modification bulletins and modern innovations are incorporated in the rejuvenation program. At right, DC-4 rudder is carefully removed for zinc chromating and recovering.

Left: During major overhaul of Northwest DC-4, Henry Walstrom, left, and Cliff Lundquist open skin of wing to perform major repair.

Hundreds of persons attended the September, 1947 grand opening of Northwest's huge, new complex at Seattle-Tacoma airport. The $1,350,000 hangar provides floor space for fleets of aircraft and houses headquarters of Northwest's western region. This was the first structure built on the new Puget Sound airfield.

MARTIN 202

The first of an order of 40 new Martin 202 twin-engine airliners went into Northwest service in November, 1947. The Baltimore-built airplane carried 36 passengers and had an enlarged cargo area. The 202, a replacement aircraft of the DC-3, cruised at 225 mph and boasted of such features as water-injection engines, buffet for hot meals and self-contained loading ramp in the tail. Note enlarged dorsal fin and increased dihedral in the wing. (See photo on page 90.) Close propeller ground clearance presented some problems, especially during Northwest's winter operations. NC 93043 (shown above) was the seventh 202 to be delivered to the company. Only 25 of the original order of 40 202s were delivered because of crashes.

Sunday, March 15, 1948, international representatives, Washington, D.C. officials and the news media attended the colorful National Airport christening ceremonies of a Northwest DC-4 "The Okinawa" and 202 "The Nominee", signifying Northwest Airlines' new route into the U.S. capital and linking it with the Orient and all important northern cities. The new route extension brought additional service to Cleveland and Pittsburgh, which was simultaneously recognized at those major cities.

A second major route to the Twin Cities airline system, Seattle-Portland-Honolulu, was approved after a long delay. Entrance of Northwest into regularly scheduled service between Hawaii and the Pacific Northwest states marked another great step forward. Over 2,000 friendly Islanders greeted the first flight as it landed in Honolulu, Thursday, December 2, 1948. The beautiful Pacific flight in DC-4 "Alu Manu" had followed colorful ceremonies at Seattle and Portland. Crew members of the first flight were: Captain Mal Freeburg, Captain Ralph Daniel, First Officer Merrill Kuehn, navigator Albert Krucovsky and purser Roland McPherren. The first return trip was crewed by Captain Bob Polhamus, Captain Russ McNown, First Officer L. C. McQuain, navigator Gerald Valesky, purser Gilland Corbitt and stewardess Marilyn Spielberger.

DC-4 (above) and Martin 202 (below) with Northwest Airlines "new look." Old, famous emblem has been dropped and replaced by new logo shown here. The distinctive new red vertical fin was result of safety studies. Wide blue band on fuselage completed our national colors. Interesting photo below depicts dramatic half-century of transportation progress.

BOEING 377 STRATOCRUISER

After a prolonged delay, Northwest Airlines received delivery of the first of ten Boeing Model 377 "Stratocruisers" on June 22, 1949. The huge double-deck airliner carried 75-100 passengers and offered a spacious flight deck. Powered by four 3,500 hp Pratt & Whitney engines, it cruised at 300+ mph and had a range of 4,600 miles. A complete galley, "his and hers" washrooms and a plush lower deck lounge were the ultimate in passenger comfort. The first two Stratocruisers were placed on the Twin-Cities-Chicago run in late July, 1949, and were dispersed over the entire system as the aircraft were delivered. Above is N74608 (No. 708).

Right: Dean J. Hanscom, western region traffic manager, left, and R. O. Bullwinkel, Northwest vice president of traffic, graphically show the size of the company's new Boeing as it is about to be delivered. John Deveny photo.

Left: Partial view of Stratocruiser's spacious passenger compartment; comfortable seats featured many advancements for the air traveler.

Above: A big day it was for Seattle, Tacoma and Northwest Airlines when the great new Seattle-Tacoma Airport (Sea-Tac) was dedicated July 9, 1949. A special feature of the program was the christening of the Stratocruiser "Seattle-Tacoma" (N64602) by Mrs. William M. Allen, wife of the president of Boeing Airplane Company. Above photo taken later gives the viewer an idea of the size of the multi-million dollar terminal.

At a 1950 region station operator's meeting are (L-R) D. C. (Dave) Evans, Eastern; Ed Leonard, Central; R. C. Anderson, Northwest superintendent; Waldo Hollingsworth, Orient; A. T. (Art) Petersen, Western.

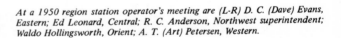

With the outbreak of hostilities in Korea, Northwest was named a prime contractor in the Military Air Transport Service. As United Nation's troops fight for survival on Korea's beaches, Northwest increased the tempo of its "airlift" flights over the Great Circle route to the Far East. Here a group of 14 Navy nurses and nine hospitalmen begin the first section of their trip to the Orient on company Stratocruiser "Tokyo." They are part of several hundred hospital personnel who are being flown to the war theater.

Chapter 6 – NORTHWEST FLIES TURBULENT SKIES

With the entire fleet of Northwest's Stratocruisers in operation, gratifying results offset the long delivery delay. Increased daily utilization, high-average passenger loads and enthusiastic acceptance by the traveling public sent company optimism soaring. The plush Boeings were flying coast-to-coast, to Alaska and Hawaii, and service extension was planned to Washington, D.C. and the Orient.

Then, for the second time in the company's history, they suffered a series of sub-standard equipment crashes. In January, 1951, the sixth Martin 202 crashed. The first occurred in 1948 and five tragically in the last ten months of 1950. The 202s were removed from service and the company's carefully planned post-war equipment program was scuttled. Three DC-3s and six DC-4s were placed back in service to fill the newly created gap, but schedules predicated on the fast Martins fell far short of practicability. For the first time, public confidence in the company was affecting sales.

President Hunter, as was his practice — good news or bad, communicated with the entire company in a personal message which said in part, " . . . We must remember that our company became an outstanding airline because it was built on sound foundations and, in the past, it has met and overcome many obstacles. It is important now that you remember your company's history and the manner in which it has grown and developed into one of the world's great domestic and international airline systems. It is my sincere belief that, with the continued help and cooperation of all of us, the year 1951 may well be one of the most successful years in our company's history . . ."

In 1951, the company continued as the prime contract on the "Korean Airlift." Two Northwest DC-4s and five DC-4s, leased from other airlines and flown by Northwest pilots, integrated their operations without conflict of commercial schedules.

In Tokyo, October, 1951, the 25th anniversary of the Twin Cities airline, an agreement with the 1,500 mile, intra Japan airline, Nippon Koku Kabu Shikikaisha, was contracted in which Northwest undertook the line's operations helping to establish the Japanese carrier. Northwest flew and maintained the aircraft while the line's own personnel handled sales, established fares, ticketing and advertising. As Japanese participation expanded, Northwest trained Japanese pilots and maintenance crews.

Back in the United States, Northwest made an important move of its La Guardia Field, N.Y. station to New York International Field at Idlewild in December, 1951.

Early in 1952, an agreement of merger was entered into by officials of Northwest Airlines, Inc. and officials of Capital Airlines, Inc. It was felt that the joining of the two systems would result in increased strength, efficiency and earning power and benefit all shareholders of both companies. The merger was vetoed by Northwest stockholders at an annual meeting in St. Paul in May, 1952. The vote was 716,835 in favor of the plan and 167,995 opposed; more than 300,000 shares were not voted. A two-thirds affirmative vote of the total outstanding stock was required by Minnesota corporate laws. One of the major oppositions to the proposal was the fear that the main base of operations might be moved out of the Twin Cities.

In the Twin Cities on April 5, 1952, the first annual dinner of the Northwest Airlines' Twenty Year Club was held honoring two decades of service of President Hunter and 45 others. Oldest employee on the roster was Louis E. Koerner, manager of maintenance, who first came aboard Northwest August 8, 1928. The bit of nostalgia and meeting of old-timers was marred days later when 700 employees waged a stubborn and resourceful fight to save Northwest's main base operations at Holman Field against the worst flood of the Mississippi River on record. Working around the clock, some employees toiled continuously for 48 hours and more filling sand bags and diking. 300 truckloads of sand, 200,000 feet of lumber and hundreds of tools and pieces of equipment were pressed into use to save Northwest's huge hangars containing millions of dollars worth of machinery, stores, aircraft parts and delicate instruments. A Douglas DC-4, which was partly dismantled, could not be moved. It was

Opposite: Northwest stewardesses and maintenance personnel assist the photographer in demonstrating the size of the company's new Boeing Stratocruiser. John R. Deveny photo.

jacked-up and sat through the rising waters. A DC-3, its overhaul job rushed to a finish, was flown from the field by Northwest test pilot E. J. "Red" Fowler.

The half-mile, five-foot dike around the overhaul base held back the angry torrent, but water entered the north hangar after the cement flooring buckled from the tremendous pressure underneath. The battle continued in the best tradition of devoted Northwest Airlines' employees until the flood eased off. The holocaust cost the company over $200,000 in protective measures and caused indirect losses from interrupted operations estimated at $350,000.

Northwest employees and officials were further saddened early in September, 1952, when they learned of the death of Col. Louis H. Brittin, founder of their company.

On the heels of this news, it was announced by President Hunter that Gen. Harold R. Harris, vice president in charge of Pan American Airways' Atlantic division, would join Northwest January 1, 1953, as president of the company. Croil Hunter was to become chairman of the board.

At a January, 1954 meeting of the board of directors, one year after Harris took the reins of Northwest, it was announced that the new chief executive was granted an "indefinite leave of absence," due to a sudden illness. Malcolm S. Mackay, vice president of the airline's continental division, was named acting president. There had been numerous reports that since Harris took over, he and some stockholders and members of the board favored moving Northwest's main base of operations out of the Twin Cities. There was further speculation that a Mackay-backed group held to keeping the airline's main base in the Twin Cities.

The Board authorized treasurer L. S. Holstad to write to the Metropolitan Airports Commission requesting a 60-day extension of the MAC's March, 1953 offer to build and finance a $12-15 million base at Wold-Chamberlain Field. In a show-down involving a Wall Street mystery man, who had been quoted as scuttling the Northwest-Capital merger, Harris resigned effective March 3, 1954. Also involved was a multi-million dollar purchase of new aircraft, in which an order for six Lockheed Super Constellations was included.

The embers of Northwest's power struggle were still glowing when the death of Rosie Stein was learned. The second great of Northwest's formidable days had passed to the great beyond as if to avoid the turmoil of present company-troubled skies. Paradoxically, Miss Stein used to answer inquiring newsmen about airline conditions the same, "Everything's rosy!"

Everything began to appear rosy when 42-year-old aviation veteran, Donald W. Nyrop, stepped jauntily out of a Northwest Stratocruiser at Wold-Chamberlain airport to assume the company's presidency in August, 1954. Nyrop told the waiting press, "Northwest is a very good airline. It serves a lot of good areas — including the Orient. It has a good background and future." He continued, "I'm looking forward to this job, in fact, I'm enthusiastic about it!"

The Elgin, Nebraska native and lawyer was highly qualified in his statements, having served as a chairman of the Civil Aeronautics Board in 1951 and 1952, and prior to that, administrator of the Civil Aeronautics Administration.

The nation's youngest president of a major airline waded into the multitude of problems confronting the company with a ten-hour day, including weekends. One of the major problems was equipment. President Nyrop ferreted five much-in-demand Douglas DC-6Bs from other airlines and sold two of the six no longer needed Lockheed Super Constellations ordered under Harris' presidency.

Three months into his job, Nyrop spoke with enthusiasm and pride when he discussed some of Northwest's achievements in a luncheon speech, bare of platitudes, to the Minneapolis Chamber of Commerce in January, 1955. "Northwest Airlines is the only airline in the United States that doesn't owe a dime," he concluded.

With the aid of Chambers of Commerce throughout Northwest's systems and support from a Minnesota Congressional delegation, led by Senator Thye and Representative Judd, permanent route certification to Anchorage and the Orient was granted to Northwest. After befuddled government footballing of route sanction to Hawaii by Northwest Airlines and Pan American Airways, Northwest was granted a three-year extension to their Seattle-Portland-Honolulu run.

The clouds began to disperse and blue sky appeared ahead for the Twin Cities airline as Nyrop asserted, "We are moving in the right direction to building one of the finest fleets of any airline, and Northwest Airlines is very fortunate in the kind of people it has, many of them with long experience."

Right: A link with home was the significance given this Northwest Airlines sign found by two un-identified U.S. Marines, who were among the United Nations forces which swept into Korea and recaptured Kimpo Airport on the outskirts of Seoul. The sign was the only object found intact on the airfield, which was reduced to a mass of rubble by repeated bombings and shellings by both armies to keep the strategic field inoperative. Acme News Pictures, Tokyo Bureau.

With Northwest Airlines in its 25th year of operations, the two oldest employees in point of service, stationed at Seattle are Clarence "Nippy" Opsahl, left, and his brother Alvin (Al) Opsahl. The two Opsahls have had colorful careers as mechanics, stunt pilots and growing with Northwest. Al learned to fly in 1928, five years before his brother. Both began as mechanics with the company at the Twin Cities; Al in September, 1928, and Nippy in April, 1929. Nippy learned to fly in 1933 and became a Northwest co-pilot in 1935, one of the few pilots in the early days to come from ground crews. Three years later he made captain and, in 1951, skippered flights to Hawaii. Al was supervising inspector at Seattle-base operations for Northwest. Opsahl photo.

Welcome to the United States! Al Piepcras, Orient region comptroller, left; Don King, Orient region manager; and William Stern, director of Northwest Airlines, greet Tokio Inove on arrival from Tokyo to attend school in America under sponsorship of Stern.

Commemorating the silver anniversary of Northwest, the Smith twins, Les, left, and Lee, flew the first Stratocruiser christened "The Washington Express" from the Twin Cities to Washington, D.C. Vice President Alben Barkley was one of the distinquished passengers. Ceremonies were conducted at both ends of the flight. Other crew members were John R. Deveny, flight engineer, and twin stewardesses Beverly and Marvl Brady.

Below: January, 1952 Northwest labor negotiating team during closing session at St. Paul. Standing: (L-R) Norris Jackson, director of labor relations, flight; Vince Doyle, co-pilot representative; Homer R. Kinney, assistant director of labor relations, flight; Mel Swanson; Dick O'Neill; Dudley Cox; Les Smith; Al Henderson; Ken Linville; Gene Markham; Chet Eklund. Seated: (L-R) Frank Judd, vice president; Linus C. Glotzbach, vice president, personnel; Jack C. Christie, representative, Air Line Pilots Association.

Right: Death took Col. Louis H. Brittin September 4, 1952 at the age of 75. The founder and former executive vice president of Northwest Airways, Inc. died in Washington, D.C. Brittin, a native of Connecticut and a West Point graduate, came to the Twin Cities area shortly before World War I and set up a branch plant for General Electric Co. After returning from the service, reportedly in the Artillery, he was instrumental in the use of power at the dam near the Twin Cities Ford plant. After he resigned from Northwest in 1934, Brittin maintained his interest in aviation as an air transport consultant and also as a member of the executive board of the aviation section of the New York Board of Trade.

Harold R. Harris, left, assumed Northwest Airlines' presidency on January 1, 1953. Harris began a military career in 1916 as an engineering officer of the First Provisional Aero Squadron at Monterey, California. During World War I, he was one of a group of American flyers sent to Italy for Caproni bomber operations. From 1920 to 1925, he was an Army test pilot and in 1922, he made the world's first emergency parachute jump from an airplane. At one time in 1926, he held 13 world flying records. During WWII, he was chief of staff of the Air Transport Command with the rank of brigadier general. President Harris resigned under fire in March, 1954.

DOUGLAS DC-6B

Northwest leased its first DC-6B in September, 1953, and placed it on its Honolulu route in mid-November. The big Douglas was a modernized, enlarged version of the time-tested DC-4. It carried 64-76 passengers in a pressurized cabin boasting the latest in passenger and crew conveniences. Powered by four 2,500 HP Pratt & Whitney engines, the ship cruised at 315 MPH at 22,400 feet and carried a crew of 5-7. Northwest eventually had 25 DC-6Bs in service and the first seven were converted "A" models. Above in-flight photo is N572 (No. 672) and features a radar nose dome. Right: Huge 117 feet, 5-inch wingspan gave the new Douglas beautiful aerodynamic stability. Below: Note absence of radar nose on N34957 (No. 657) as a DC-6A. This ship, the first DC-6, was leased and later purchased by Northwest.

Alaska and Northwest Airlines salutes the 50th anniversary of powered
flight and the dedication of Anchorage International Airport in December,
1953. Right: Part of crowd, numbered in the thousands, that attended the
grand opening of the huge, modern airdrome located south of Anchorage.
Control tower, right, collapsed to rubble during disasterous Good Friday
earthquake in 1964. Above: Northwest DC-6B, N566 (No. 666), at
Anchorage International Airport signifies transfer of company operations
from their old home at Elmendorf Air Force Base. Anchorage, "The Air
Crossroads of the World," served many international and Alaska air
carriers.

Left: Alaska Senior Senator Bob Bartlett, right, receives congratulations
from Northwest Airline's vice president of the Orient region, Don King, on
the new Anchorage International Airport. Senator Bartlett, a protege of,
and in 1944, successor to Alaska Delegate to the U.S. Congress Anthony J.
Dimond, was actively engaged in pioneer development of air commerce in
Alaska.

In July, 1954, Northwest Airlines deactivated its fueling base at flat, treeless Shemya Island, (in photo at right), located 35 miles from the western end of the Aleutian chain, and switched its trans-Pacific operations to Cold Bay Airport located at the tip of the Alaska Peninsula. Northwest had been using Shemya as a refueling stop since 1947.

Left: Albert G. Redpath of New York, widely known in financial, legal and education circles, was named a member of Northwest Airline's board of directors in December, 1951. In August, 1953, many Northwest friends and associates were shocked by the death of board member William T. Gardiner. A board member since 1945, Gardiner was killed in a crash of his private plane. The former twice-governor of Maine was a WWII hero, having received the Legion of Merit and several other distinguished awards. 1954 board members, in addition to Redpath, were Croil Hunter, chairman; James H. Binger, Morton H. Fry, Robert M. Hardy, Joseph T. Johnson, Malcolm S. Mackay, Alonzo Petteys, C. Frank Reavis, William Stern, Albert F. Tegen, Lyman E. Wakefield, Jr., Albert J. Weatherhead, Jr. and Wheelock Whitney. In 1954, Northwest employees numbered 5,000. Below: 1954 route system map of Northwest.

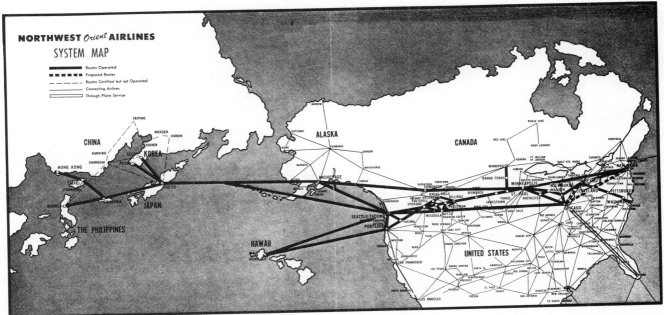

Donald W. Nyrop was elected president of Northwest Airlines in October, 1954, after having been engaged in private law practice in Washington, D.C. He was chairman of the Civil Aeronautics Board in 1951 and 1952. Nyrop was born in Elgin, Nebraska, in 1912 and graduated from Doane College at Crete, Nebraska. He received his law degree from George Washington University. In 1942, he became special assistant to the chairman of the CAB. From 1942 to 1946, he served with the Air Transport Command of the Army Air Force. He attained the rank of lieutenant colonel and earned tne distinguished Legion of Merit. In 1948, he became deputy administrator of the Civil Aeronautics Administration. By Presidential appointment, he served as administrator of the Civil Aeronautics Administration. At 42, Nyrop became the youngest president of a U.S. major airline when he assumed the post.

Below is Lockheed artist's conception of how Northwest new Lockheed 1049-G Super Constellation will look when delivered in early 1955. Originally, six of these aircraft were purchased under President Harris. Under President Nyrop's updating of the company's system, the "Connies" were not needed; two were sold.

In keeping with fashion trends, Northwest stewardesses donned this new uniform in mid-1954. Stewardess Georgia Murphy gracefully models fashion designer Tina Leser's creation.

Left: Former Twin Cities chief radio operator Robert Kuehn demonstrates latest Northwest communications equipment.

100,000th GI flown on Northwest's Korean airlift, Corporal DeAngelos, receives welcome home from stewardesses Pat Stickel, left, and Jan Heisler.

LOCKHEED 1049-G SUPER CONSTELLATION

Powered by four Wright Turbo Compound engines, the four "Connies" were placed exclusively in international operations. The luxurious planes offered Northwest air travelers the finest and latest service between the United States, the Orient and to Hawaii. Northwest's first 1049-G Super Constellation was named "Hawaiian Express." Placement of the new Lockheeds in Pacific service enabled the company to utilize additional Boeing Stratocruisers in service on its trans-continental route system.

Above: The first Lockheed 1049-G Super Constellation to be delivered to Northwest, N5172V (No. 172), takes off from Burbank Airfield, California. Note wing tip fuel tanks commonly referred to as "Tokyo tanks."

Photo below of N5172V shows the size of the 60-100 passenger "Connie." Cruise speed at 20,000 feet was 300 mph with top speed over 350 mph. A crew of seven operated the dependable bird.

Forty-three passengers boarded Northwest Orient Airlines' first Turbo Constellation flight at Seattle-Tacoma International Airport February 15, 1955, for Anchorage. A couple of real Northwest veterans, Captains Walter Bullock and Fred Zimmerly, skippered the flight. Crew members included: Rudy Dahl, first officer; Chris Priebe, flight engineer; Art Stevens, flight service attendant; Kay Tigges and Alice Anderson, stewardesses.

Who says elephants can't fly? At right, "Miss Bell," a 1,000 pound two-year-old Siamese elephant is forklifted aboard a Northwest DC-4 freighter for her trip to Anchorage. The pachyderm was a last-minute replacement for a no-show act at the northern city's Shrine Circus. Miss Bell was allowed to familiarize herself with the big Douglas and airport surroundings before boarding, under the watchful eye of her trainer, Terrell Jacobs. Sedatives were administered before she returned to her crate. Through the years, Northwest has flown animals of all descriptions.

Two of Northwest's best-known pilots and their wives were killed in the crash of a private plane October 10, 1955. The two couples, Captain and Mrs. Donald J. King and Captain and Mrs. Charles W. Ryan, were returning to Prior Lake, Minnesota, near the Twin Cities, after a hunting and fishing trip in Canada. The plane crashed on the farm of Edwin Smith, former Northwest Airlines' pilot.

King, shown at left, was a native of Sodus, Michigan. He joined Northwest as a co-pilot in 1937. King served Northwest in many administrative and executive capacities during his career, including those of chief pilot, eastern region superintendent of operations, northern region operations superintendent during WWII and vice president of the Orient region. He had 11,553 flying hours to his credit when he died at the age of 46.

Charlie Ryan, 43, was a native of Lake City, Florida. He joined Northwest as a co-pilot in 1942 after serving as a military cadet flight instructor with aeronautical firms in Georgia and Florida. He had logged 13,217 hours with the company.

First "Connie" (N5175V, No. 175) to be overhauled in Northwest base at Holman Field, St. Paul, in October, 1955.

Northwest Stratocruiser, N74608, No. 608, cruises past Mount Fuji, Japan's highest peak, winging eastward signifying termination of Orient service by the venerable Boeings. DC-6Bs and Connies assumed flights of the Pacific operation while the Stratocruisers handled domestic routes.

Left: Northwest Orient Airlines personnel stationed at the new Okinawa ticket office in 1955. At right is station manager Lou Devantees.

Below: Grand-opening ceremonies of Northwest's new offices in Okinawa. Note office of Japan Air Lines to the left of Northwest's. Japan Air Lines was fostered by the Twin Cities airline.

Chapter 7 – A NEW HOME IN THE TWIN CITIES

Northwest's equipment problems and organizational upheavals of the early 1950's were all but forgotten in 1956, as more pressurized Douglas DC-6Bs were placed in service and President Nyrop demonstrated an impressive grip of the company helm. A dependable and productive fleet of Stratocruisers, Connies and Douglas DC-4 and DC-6B airliners gradually began swinging the status pendulum toward increased net profits and restored public confidence.

Continuing efforts to have the finest fleet in the industry was further indicated when an order for eight long-range Douglas DC-7Cs was placed with the successful Santa Monica aircraft firm. Technical studies and economic analyses were conducted of turboprop and jet aircraft, as the company entered into a comprehensive planning of their future major role in world air commerce.

Northwest Airlines future in the Twin Cities area was highlighted when the company entered into a long-term agreement with the Metropolitan Airports Commission (MAC) to provide a $15 million overhaul, operations and general headquarters facility at Wold-Chamberlain Field. The complex was to be constructed on a 76-acre rectangular tract of land, almost entirely in the former historical Fort Snelling area, and would be adjacent to the proposed multi-million dollar terminal and administration building of the airport itself. The final agreement and contract, revised many times, was approved by MAC members and then the voluminous document was officially signed by President Nyrop on March 5, 1956. Completion date was set for mid-1958.

By mid-1956, planning for Northwest's upcoming 30th anniversary celebration was well underway. A projected nostalgic coast-to-coast Ford Trimotor flight resulted in the location of a former Northwest "Tin Goose" (NC8419) at Johnson Flying Service in Missoula, Montana. The historic airliner was flown to the company's overhaul base at St. Paul, where it was refurbished and repainted in original Northwest colors. The October ten-day flight, piloted by big-league captains, Leon S. "Deke" DeLong and Joe Kimm, was an unqualified success, as young and old cheered the dependable Ford at 20 stops on its cross-country journey.

After the 5,500 company employees observed the airline milestone and historians duly recorded the event, Northwest continued its fleet modernization program as Douglas DC-7Cs came off the Santa Monica, California production line and were turned over to Northwest Airlines. The latest Douglas 95-passenger aircraft were placed on the Orient run, commemorating ten years service of the Great Circle route.

The DC-7s finalized transition to an all four-engine fleet as the last of the "old workhorse" DC-3s ended their extended duty and the "grand ole ladies" of the famous Douglas origin disappeared from company inventory.

On December 6, 1958, Northwest began operations on its new Florida route, providing the first through-plane service between Seattle-Tacoma, Twin Cities and other Northwest cities on the one end, and Tampa, St. Petersburg, Clearwater and Miami, on the other. The major route addition received encouraging initial traffic response. Previous to this newest system extension, Northwest had an interchange agreement with Eastern Airlines, which became effective in December, 1954, and provided through services between Miami and the Twin Cities via Chicago.

On the heels of the Florida route inauguration, the company announced DC-6B daily service to Hawaii and Winnipeg, Canada. Additionally, air-truck freight flights were extended coast-to-coast using DC-6Bs converted to versatile cargo-passenger configurations.

During 1958, contracts were awarded for the construction of the major portions of the new overhaul, operations and headquarters facility at Wold-Chamberlain Field. Construction was proceeding on schedule, with occupancy now planned for mid-1959.

With its new main base well underway, Northwest prepared for one of the benefits of

Opposite: Bird's eye view of an interesting geometric pattern of steel as construction gets well underway on Northwest Airline's $15 million general office and overhaul base at Wold-Chamberlain field. The tab came to $18 million despite trimming of non-essentials.

their comprehensive planning as ten new long-range, prop-jet Lockheed Electras were placed on coast-to-coast and Florida service. The Electras heralded Northwest Airlines' new image, termed "Imperial Service" and signified by a new imperial eagle logo painted on the vertical fin of the aircraft. Segments of the new framework included new direct service to Atlanta, Georgia, and New York to Anchorage polar flights, using DC-7C equipment.

At New York in May, 1959, contracts were let for underground work on the company's new terminal at Idlewild International Airport. A new hangar at O'Hare Field, Chicago, was in the design stage, with construction slated for the early 1960's.

As Northwest Airlines entered the sixties, optimistic forecasts were marred by a Tell City, Indiana, Electra accident, which resulted in operation restrictions of the aircraft and postponement of further deliveries, pending government approval of a modification to permit a return to normal operations.

A delay in delivery of DC-8C jet aircraft and an additional delay of inauguration of the new intercontinental Douglas airliners as a result of a pilot's dispute regarding the operational status of a third pilot's seat in July, 1960, sharply cut into the company's revenue. When the DC-8s were finally placed in service between Seattle-Tacoma and Tokyo, a flight engineer's dispute in October, 1960, grounded the aircraft for the balance of the year.

Meanwhile, transfer of maintenance and stores to the new main base at Wold-Chamberlain Field (now Minneapolis-St. Paul International Airport) was begun in July and completed in August, 1960. Construction of the General Office (GO) Building at the same location was nearing completion.

With its new headquarters and plans for an all-jet fleet, Northwest optimistically entered its 35th year of operations.

Right: A Northwest Orient Airline's Super-G Constellation made the non-stop flight from Okinawa to Tokyo in two hours, 29 minutes on January 10, 1956, to establish a new commercial speed record between those two points. Captain Walter Bullock, who set a Seoul-Tokyo record in December previous, was at the controls of the plane. The crew were Gene Markham, co-pilot; Steve Radjenovich, flight engineer; Edson (Ed) Marahrens, navigator; Rigido Vales, purser; Gloria Goitia and Evy Garcia, stewardesses. During 1956, Bullock marked his 40th year as a pilot and at the time of this record flight he had logged 30,000 hours of flying time with Northwest. He was believed to be the only commercial airline pilot still active who had been flying 40 years.

Captain Dick O'Neill and flight engineer Bob Weigel, on flight deck of Boeing Stratocruiser, check over their next flight segment. Photo taken at Washington, D.C. in July, 1956.

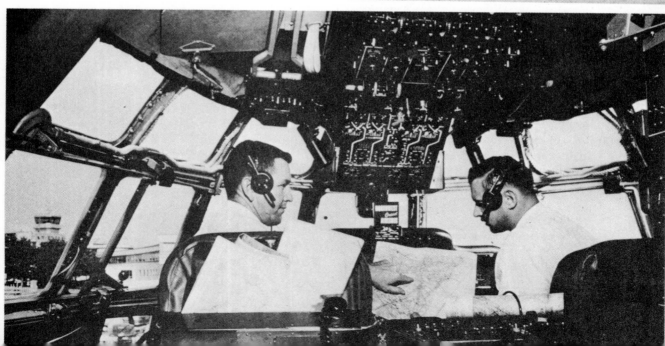

Above: Busy working on a new overhaul base shop blueprints on a table at old overhaul base are, facing camera, from left: George Moir, Northwest engineer; Phil Rich, Walter Butler engineer; Tom Albrecht and Don Kirch, Northwest engineers; Freddie Wick, Walter Butler engineer. Backs to camera: Bob Ritchie, Northwest Director of Facilities Planning; and Paul Wanshura, Walter Butler engineer.

Left: Discussing artist conception of Northwest's new main base, from the left: Bob Ritchie; Dale Merrick, assistant vice president — properties; and Rollie Chambers, director of properties.

Below: Employee ideas are being integrated into construction of new overhaul base. From the left, Don Kirch, Northwest engineer in charge of propeller shop plans and Ed Hamm, supt. of plans, equipment and engineering, confer with John Rataczak, propeller shop crew chief, and Joe Schuster, propeller shop mechanical supervisor, about their shop's layout.

Above: Home after 22 years, Ford Trimotor N8419 rolls out for engine run-up after complete refurbishing at Northwest's St. Paul overhaul base. The Ford was sold by the company in 1935 to Northern Air Transport, Inc., Fairbanks, Alaska. From 1936 to 1938, she was owned by Wien Alaska Airways and in 1940-41, Star Airlines, Inc., Anchorage, claimed ownership. Information is sketchy until 1945 when Monroe Airways, Inc., Monroe, Michigan, held title to the early-day airliner. In 1950, new ownership transferred her to a berth with Johnson Flying Service, Missoula, Montana, from whom Northwest leased the airplane for this occasion. George Holey photo.

30TH ANNIVERSARY

N8419 took to the airways again in October, 1956, as part of Northwest Orient Airlines' observance of its 30th anniversary. Northwest's coast-to-coast flight took ten days, with 20 stops for brief inspections of the old Ford by young and old alike. Ceremonies and crew interviews were held all along the route. In an effort to illustrate the tremendous advances in commercial aviation since Northwest was founded in 1926, two of Northwest's veteran captains flew the plane; Captain Deke DeLong of St. Paul, Northwest's senior pilot, and Captain Joe Kimm of Seattle. DeLong joined Northwest in 1928; Kimm began in 1929 and was a co-pilot aboard Northwest's famed western transcontinental flight from the Twin Cities to Seattle in 1933. Other crew members on the anniversary flight included Walt Kollath, early-day Northwest mechanic, who said all he had to do to the old Ford was gas and oil her; she performed beautifully. Coral Yahr was the stewardess. DeLong and Kimm were spelled off on the Twin Cities-Chicago-Twin Cities segment by Captain Mel Swanson and Captain Bob Bean. Kimm said "There were two fascinating things about the old Trimotor; noise, and its ability to climb. We cruised at 85 mph; when we put on more power, it would just start to climb." In New York, when DeLong and Kimm arrived from the Twin Cities to begin the coast-to-coast flight, Kimm met his wife at their hotel. Mrs. Kimm told him to stop shouting, everyone in the lobby was staring at them! While in New York, DeLong and Kimm were featured on "Arthur Godfrey Time" TV and radio shows.

Below: Governor Walter J. Kohler of Wisconsin (second from left) met the Trimotor when it landed at Madison. He is shown with Captain Joe Kimm, left, and Malcolm Mackay, Northwest's executive vice president, and Captain "Deke" DeLong, right. Veterans DeLong and Kimm had to "check-out" in the Trimotor for CAA type certification, which included complex modern procedures not applicable to the "Tin Goose."

Above: Pioneer Northwest Airlines' employees M. E. Andersen, left, and R. C. (Andy) Anderson, pose beside N8419 as they recall the early days of the Twin Cities airline.

Below: N8419 at Midway Field, Chicago. In background is grand-daughter Stratocruiser, N74602 (No. 702).

Above: Douglas DC-7C, N284 (No. 284), was the fourth DC-7C to be delivered to Northwest in the spring of 1957. A total of 17 were in Northwest service.

DOUGLAS DC-7C

Northwest announced the first of the Douglas DC-7C equipment was slated for its trans-Pacific route April 28, 1957. Three planes will provide four weekly route-trips between Seattle-Tacoma and Manila, via Tokyo and Okinawa, in combination first-class, tourist configuration. The DC-7C was an aircraft designed to carry the best performance of piston-driven airliners right into the jet era. Northwest received delivery of 17 DC-7Cs during 1957 and 1958. Among airplanes of various types, the big, new Douglas was characterized by its speed, carrying capacity and long range. Seating capacity ranged from 96 in five abreast-tourist to 72 first-class.

Above: DC-7C "Seven Seas", so named because it was the first truly intercontinental airliner, first plane to have range for full-load, non-stop coast-to-coast capabilities. Ship shown here is N285 (No. 285).

Northwest Airlines' "new" NEWS is shown at left. Several changes in format, most self-evident, had been effected, beginning with this February, 1957 issue. Color on front and back covers, standard since April, 1952, had been eliminated and the size reduced for easier handling. Robert Lee Johnson was editor of the publication in 1957.

Northwest's fleet of DC-6Bs began sporting shiny new propeller spinners in April, 1957, as seen in photo above of N572 (No. 672). The "new look" spinners are quite an advantage; improved engine cooling, increased aircraft speed and protecting hub dome oil from congealing during cold-weather operations. Being a hydramatic propeller, pitch changing is dependent on oil in the hub drum.

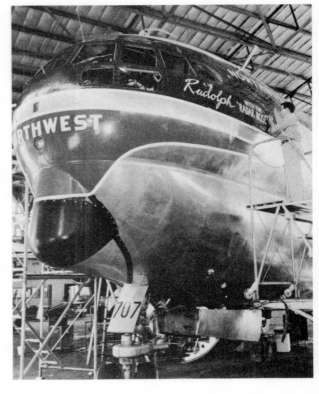

Above: Northwest mechanic Bud Morgan dubs first radar equipped company Stratocruiser, "Rudolph with the Radar Nose." Entire Northwest pressurized fleet soon carried Bendix dual-scope X band radar. John R. Deveny photo.

Left: "Miss Northwest Airlines," Janet Chi, left, presents bouquet to Northwest Captain Bill Wallace. The ceremony was, in part, a recognition of Northwest Airlines' 10th anniversary of service to the Orient and recognition of new DC-7C airliners which Wallace flew to this Taipei airport as part of Northwest's goodwill tour. Miss Chi is a secretary for CAT (Civil Air Transport), Taipei. Gentleman in the center is Joe Sykes, Northwest Airlines' sales representative.

Right: October, 1957, Northwest Airlines board meeting held at the Bishop National Bank, Honolulu, Hawaii. (L-R) James H. Binger, Ted R. Gamble, Lyman E. Wakefield, Jr., Joseph T. Johnson, William Stern, Albert G. Redpath, Donald W. Nyrop, chairman Croil Hunter, A. E. (Ed) Floan, Malcolm S. Mackay, Alonzo Petteys, Clyde B. Morgan and Morton H. Fry.

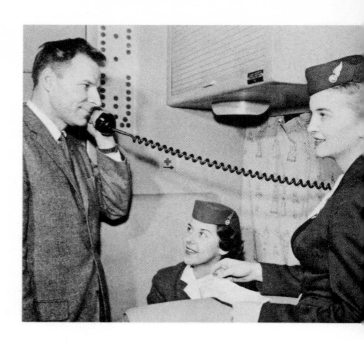

Above is Director of Communications R. H. Weihe, overseer of Northwest's first air-ground communications. Right: Bob Glischinski, superintendent of radio communications, puts through a call to a resident phone in the Twin Cities from a radio-phone installation aboard a Stratocruiser. Stewardesses Robbins and Joan Winterquist look on.

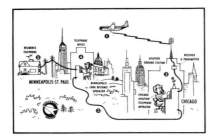

"Sky-truck" freight service, which Northwest pioneered in conjunction with 19 motor carriers in the Midwest area, was extended to the Pacific Northwest late in 1958. Since the service was inaugurated in November, 1957, it had been a boon to merchants who wished to ship swiftly to and from larger cities in the East served by Northwest. Meantime, air cargo was an important growing segment of Northwest Airlines, under the supervision of Tom Nolan, air freight director. Nolan, who started with Northwest as a bus driver in July, 1937, had 19 years experience in the air cargo and transportation field in 1958. He has held several important administrative positions with the company including superintendent of cargo, superintendent of aircraft movement, chief clerk and assistant to the mail and express traffic manager. Above: Cargo being off-loaded at Anchorage, Alaska.

"The gang's all here!" (L-R) Herman Lerdahl, Ed Bolton, Earle Hale, Russ McNown, Hugh Rueschenberg and Earl "Whitey" Stein. Hilsen photo.

In June, 1958, a horse named "Hakuchikara," reputed to be Japan's fastest, arrived from Tokyo at Seattle-Tacoma airport for a U.S. racing schedule. The five-year-old thoroughbred was owned by Mr. Hiroshi Nishi of Tokyo, in black suit in photo at left. Grandsire is of British stock, but both stud and mare were born in Japan.

Right: Hakuchikara's trainer, Reikichi Ishida, and Dr. Leon K. Jones, U.S. quarantine inspector. Mr. Nishi used a dummy airplane wing and doorway with recordings of airplane engines to prepare the horse for the ride. He was loaded into the plane with a crane.

125

"Two-bits on this one, Don!" A little, relaxed sidewalk shuffleboard during lunch break at old G. O. (L-R) Don Carlson, Bill Diehl, Del Severance, Roger Nielsen, Fred Smith, Beryl White, Stu Lee and Pete Patzke.

Right: Construction work underway at new G. O. site, Wold-Chamberlain Field, in the spring of 1958.

End of an era for Northwest Airlines — no more DC-3s. Expressions from Northwest captains like . . . "She was, and is, a grand old girl" . . . "A fine, reliable, trustworthy airplane" . . . were echoed with the phasing out of the old workhorse of 19 years with Northwest. The company's last DC-3 flight (N39544, No. 344) landed at Seattle-Tacoma airport at 11:28 p.m. September 27, 1958. Above is ship N45333 (No. 349) in company colors at time of retirement. Left: "Old No. 1" NC21711 was sold in October, 1949. She spent nearly four years in the air, carried some 200,000 passengers and had a change-over of 50 pairs of engines. Originally purchased for $125,000, "Old No. 1" sold for $25,000.

Above: New $5,800,000 air terminal at the Portland International Airport. Right: Beautiful terminal building at Logan Field, Billings, Montana, in the summer of 1958. Airport modernization programs were clear indication of tremendous increase of air travel on Northwest ports of call.

"It may seem geographically incorrect, but now you can fly Northwest to Florida," stated the Northwest Airlines Jan-Feb '59 News, when after years of effort, a north-south route was awarded. The temperature was three below zero when Captain Skelly Wright, left, took off in Stratocruiser No. 704 from the Twin Cities December 6, 1958, and headed south. When he and co-pilot Herb Ewald landed at Miami International Airport six hours later, it was 80 degress under sunny skies. Stewardess Marcia Archibald donned an Alaska parka prior to boarding, but brought her swim suit for Miami attire. Check pilot on the flight was Captain Jack Redmond. Ed Wheat was flight engineer.

Northwest's retiring senior pilot, Captain "Deke" DeLong, was greeted by his fellow pilots (above) on his arrival at the Twin Cities from his last flight to Winnipeg, Canada, in March, 1959. DeLong's 40-year flying career included 30 years with Northwest, commencing in 1928. He had participated in many firsts with the Twin Cities airline and was the only pilot with Northwest to fly to the age of 65.

Right: DeLong tells a couple of early-day yarns to fellow Northwest veteran captains. (L-R) Curt Davis, Les Wagner, Lee Smith, DeLong, Bert Ritchie.

Below: Early 1930's photo of Ford Trimotor piloted by Captain DeLong and being loaded for St. Paul-Chicago flight. Ron Stelzig is passenger agent at "Tin Goose" doorway.

First incoming passengers, right, following the official dedication of the $300,000 modern NAHA Civil Air Terminal, above, on May 9, 1959. Passengers from Northwest Airlines' Imperial Service are shown entering the terminal as Northwest station manager Gordon Gralund (right) looks on. The DC-7C (left background), flying from Manila, Taipei to Tokyo and the U.S., made a special stop at Okinawa in honor of the terminal opening.

The shape of things to come is evident in aerial photo above, as Northwest's new $18,000,000 system-wide general office and overhaul base at Wold-Chamberlain field is taking shape. Overhaul and maintenance hangars are nearing completion (center right) as the new airport terminal building construction (lower left) gets well underway. The amount of utilities needed to support Northwest's base — water, electricity, gas, etc. — could support a city of 10,000 persons. Right: President Nyrop makes an on-the-scene inspection of overhaul base construction progress as he confers with ironworker Larry Matson, left, of Western Steel Erection Company.

129

Northwest's first "Polar Imperial" flight, non-stop to Anchorage and one-stop to Tokyo, left New York City June 6, 1959. The new service furnishes eastern seaboard residents with their first non-stop service to Alaska and with fastest, only through-plane service between the East coast and the Orient. Left: At Anchorage, former Fur Rendezvous queen Rita Gravel, puts "lei" of Fur Rendezvous buttons on Captain E. J. "Red" Fowler, who skippered Flight No. 99, New York-Anchorage segment of first "Polar Imperial" non-stop flight. Flight departed five minutes late and arrived on the minute as published in schedule. Flight time was 13 hours, two minutes. Other crew members of the Douglas DC-7C, N285 (No. 285), were Captain Ron McLaughlin, First Officer Herb Ewald, flight engineers Dick Frye and Wes Brum, and check pilot (and chief pilot at the time) Don Shafer.

Right: N8419 in "airplane heaven." One of Northwest's original Ford Trimotors, which was refurbished and flown across the United States in 1956 to help celebrate the airline's 30th anniversary, is no longer flying. The doughty, little "Tin Goose" was making a landing approach to a remote Forest Service landing strip at Moose Creek, high in the Montana Rockies in July, 1959, when a tricky crosswind sent her beyond the airstrip limits into a bank of fuel storage drums. N8419 was "washed out." Appreciation to Mr. Jack R. Hughes, general manager, Johnson Flying Service, Missoula, and efforts of Mr. Albin C. Hammond, air operations specialist, Region 1, U.S. Forest Service. Photo courtesy of U.S. Forest Service, Nezperce National Forest.

Left: DC-6B simulator, valued at $300,000, was purchased by Northwest and put into service September, 1959. The simulator, to train pilots, although expensive, realizes a substantial savings compared to high cost in-flight training. Captain J. H. (Jerry) Kilian, left, discusses simulator procedures with Captain F. E. (Fred) Wharton. Kilian joined Northwest August 1, 1944; Wharton began with the company May 17, 1943. Vice President Frank C. Judd also announced purchase of $1 million DC-8 simulator to be delivered in 1960.

LOCKHEED L-188 "ELECTRA"

The Lockheed L-188 "Electra," a completely new airplane, was an important part of Northwest's bid for newest and fastest equipment in the industry. Powered by four 3,750 HP Allison engines, the Electra had a designed cruise speed of 400+ mph. Some of the new features of the bird included radiant heating, power-operated self-contained loading stairs, two galleys and a built-in beverage center. The lavishly colored passenger compartment offered up to 90 coach seating. Lockheed L-188 Electra, N130US (No. 130), above, is one of first ten ships delivered in 1959. The new airliners were placed immediately in coast-to-coast and Florida service.

Above: Ken Hove of Northwest Airlines, right, accepts delivery of the company's first Electra from Lockheed's Jim Shires. Northwest officially entered the "jet age" at 9:15 p.m. July 25, 1959, when the airline's first Electra touched down at Wold-Chamberlain Field. The delivery crew, Captain Paul Soderlind, superintendent of flight standards; Captain Ralph Render, supervisor of flight training; George Dahl, superintendent of flight engineers; and Steve Hanto, check and training flight engineer, were enthusiastic about Northwest's new "baby."

Right: First Northwest Electra, N121US (No. 121), at Lockheed factory, displays Imperial Eagle logo on vertical fin, symbolic of Northwest's new Imperial Service commensurate with all-jet fleet, Electras and to-be-delivered Douglas DC-8 aircraft.

Left: Organ music aloft. Organist C. R. "Swanney" Swanson, Minneapolis, plays favorite melody for George Grimm, left, Minneapolis Tribune columnist, in a Northwest Airlines' experiment conducted aboard Stratocuriser No. 709, late in 1959. The music in the sky, piped through six enlarged speakers throughout the airliner, was apparently successful with contented Northwest air traveler at right.

Stewardess graduating class, July 8, 1960. Front row: (L-R) Harriet Meyer, Karen Peterson, Jane Benson, Teddy Skrove, Doris Skeffes, Carol Heppensfal, Connie Schmidt. Back row: Carolyn Metz, Patricia Hess, Gwendolyn Kablitz, Jeanne Lind, Carol Greeley, Judith Winterbotham, Betty Chu.

Left: Frank C. Judd, maintenance and station operations vice president, announced in early 1960, Northwest Airlines will be the first carrier to receive Douglas DC-8s with the advanced model Pratt & Whitney JT4A-9 engine. Judd joined Northwest as a co-pilot in 1931, made captain in 1935, and during WW-II, he was superintendent of the airline's northern and western regions. In 1945, he was western region manager and a year later, vice president for the western region. Between 1951 and 1960, Judd served as vice president for operations, vice president in charge of maintenance and station operations. In 1961, he was promoted to vice president of maintenance and engineering, the office he holds as of this writing. He is a native of Minneapolis.

Last of the Stratocruisers. The venerable Boeing Model 377 Stratocruiser ushered in an age of luxury air transportation. Northwest, last U.S. scheduled operator of Stratocruisers on domestic runs, removed them from service September 15, 1960. They had been in service 11 years, one month and two weeks. The big airliner was expensive to operate, but served well for the company and had a loyal following. Northwest pilots generally summed up the "Strato" as stable and "honest." Fifty-six Stratocruisers were delivered to six U.S. and European airlines, of which Northwest had ten, N74601 to N74610. Two were lost: N74607 burned in an April 14, 1959 fire while parked on a Minneapolis ramp and N74608, shown in photo at right, was lost in Puget Sound April 2, 1956.

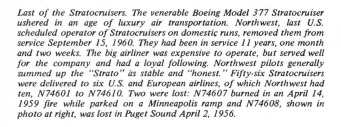

Above: Included in the move to the new overhaul base is fuselage of Hamilton Metalplane shown here. Despite markings, the bird (NC875H) was not one owned by Northwest. It is currently being restored by Jack Lysdale of the Twin Cities.

Moving day at Northwest. On July 6-7, 1960, eight semi-trailer trucks left the old home at St. Paul's Holman Field before dawn for Wold-Chamberlain field, loaded down with steel aircraft maintenance docks and other equipment. The eight truck caravans, under police escort, completed the move to the new home.

Right: 6,852 people visited Northwest's "open house" at new overhaul base. The event was sponsored by Northwest's Twin Cities Management Club and the employee services division of Northwest personnel department.

With the opening of the new base, the addition of turboprop Electras and the new pure jet Douglas DC-8 intercontinental airliner, Northwest Orient Airlines looked forward to the sixties and success as a world air carrier.

Chapter 8 — END OF AN ERA — LAST OF
THE PISTONS

The labor disputes that beset Northwest Airlines in June and October, 1960, temporarily set back an anticipated full-swing into the sixties with their fleets of new turboprop Electras and pure-jet DC-8 airliners.

With the dawn of 1961, and resumption of scheduled service, the airline announced the purchase of six Seattle-built Boeing 720B medium range jet transports. The 720Bs, introduced with the more efficient and higher thrust Pratt & Whitney JT3D turbo fan, found Northwest as a prime, first customer. The company's initial enthusiasm for the fast, versatile Electras was deterred by shocking accidents. The subsequent operation restrictions, pending completion of modifications, resulted in cut-back schedules.

Secondly, the obvious commercial trend to pure-jet equipment coincided with the company's fleet modernization program. The medium Boeings would handle domestic traffic with the big Douglas intercontinental servicing the Alaska-Orient routes. As the 720Bs came off the production lines, veteran airline pilots faced with the new mandatory age 60 retirement regulation began dropping off company rosters, much to their consternation.

The first Northwest senior pilot to be affected by the new ruling was aviation pioneer Captain Walter R. Bullock. He had learned to fly in November, 1916, and had become one of the stalwarts of Northwest, contributing much to its growth and development since joining the company in September, 1927.

Opposite: Empennage section of Northwest Boeing 727-100 tri-jet symbolizing the dawn of the jet airliner era. A departure from previously designed U.S. jets, the 727 grew out of Boeing Company market studies of a modern short-to-medium-range jet to replace piston-type aircraft currently in service. First 727 rolled out of the Boeing Renton, Washington plant on November 27, 1962. Northwest has operated (and still does) twenty-eight 727s of the 100, 100C and 200 Model series. John R. Deveny photo.

Bullock's retirement illustrates the impact of the new regulation. He was on a routine trip when he heard the news that the federal decree had been ratified. After arriving at his destination, he communicated with Twin Cities company operations to verify the news report. The company official expressed doubt, stating that nothing official had reached them. Bullock took off on his return flight to Minneapolis-St. Paul.

After landing at home base, the youthful looking captain stepped lightly from his airplane and was notified that he was through; the official word had come down. In the belief that he could fly commercially for five more years, and without last flight ceremonies traditional among all airline pilots, March 15, 1961, was a bitter day for Bullock. He holds no animosity toward anyone, least of all Northwest Airlines, as he said, "They broke their backs seeing to it that everything was square with me administratively."

Earlier retirement of pilots, a large majority of whom had learned to fly when "bustin' up a crate was all in a day's work" and who had become the nucleus building the airlines, ironically were forced from the scene. They epitomized the many changes enveloping commercial aviation; larger, faster aircraft shrinking the world; impersonal computerized mass movement of air travelers; a new era in the fastest growing mode of transportation.

The changing scene did not preclude the "oldtimers" from reflecting on their career roles that made it all possible. Nostalgia took on an added significance as Northwest Airlines celebrated its 35th anniversary October 1, 1961. New and old employees alike shared in the continuance of company dedication and spirit of competitiveness.

Fierce, competitive business tactics disallowed any moments of nostalgic reflections as Northwest placed their first six new Boeing 720Bs in operation and reordered an additional three. A decision to phase out the Douglas DC-8 came in the form of a May, 1962 notice of purchase of three Boeing 707-320B long-range fan-jets with delivery set for the following November. The continuing good performance of the DC-8 notwithstanding, Northwest's time honored standardization of engines and components and interchange of airframe parts necessitated a complete swing to the well-proven successful Boeing family of jets.

Early in 1964, with the 720Bs showing encouraging net profits and the larger sister 320Bs being placed in service on the Alaska-Orient route, Northwest ordered 11 Boeing 727-100 short-to-medium-range tri-jets. The $68,800,000 order included an additional two 720Bs..

It was during this period of time that three notable figures of Northwest Airlines passed on to their reward. On January 1, 1964, William Stern, 77, a director of Northwest since 1938, died after a long illness. Stern took a close personal interest in the airlines and for some years was a special assistant to former president Croil Hunter.

Eighteen days later on January 19, J. B. "Big Jim" La Mont, 72, who retired in 1945 as superintendent of inspection, died in the Twin Cities. Besides being a pioneer mechanic with the old Northwest Airways, La Mont assisted many young men to go to work for the fast growing company and was extremely well liked by all echelons of Northwest.

The third notable figure to be missed was former senior captain L. S. "Deke" DeLong, 70, who retired in 1959. DeLong flew many first flights during his service with the company beginning in 1928.

In June, 1964, at a luncheon in Minneapolis, President Nyrop was presented a Presidential "E" by then Secretary of Agriculture Orville E. Freeman. The high award, for excellence in developing export markets, was noted by Secretary Freeman in conjunction with Northwest Airlines' direct and indirect effective efforts in keeping the nation's economy strong through its enterprising "Visit USA" campaign. The campaign brought many thousands of tourists to the United States from the Far East. Freeman, in his remarks, also recalled Northwest Airlines' Presidential "E" award program of WWII honoring manufacturing firms for outstanding contributions to the war effort.

Continued efforts by Northwest Airlines for Cleveland-Chicago service was realized when the route was inaugurated October 5, 1964. The company was awarded the route segment along with new authority between Cleveland and Philadelphia and between the latter point and Detroit by the Civil Aeronautics Board in August. Service on the latter two routes was begun April 1, 1965.

Northwest's additional routes, the success of their non-stop Seattle-Tokyo jet flights and many other long and short term planning benefits, reflected in President Nyrop's January, 1965 announcement that Northwest's 1964 growth in domestic revenue passenger miles of 25.7% surpassed industry averages of 14.3% for all carriers. Nyrop stressed the importance of increased and improved service to the public for continued success. Years like 1964 are a necessity for the future... "competition is increasing and to remain competitive, we must continue to improve the quality of our product..."

More orders for Boeing 320s, 720Bs and 727s were placed to continue the airline's equipment betterment campaign.

As the fresh-from-the-factory Boeings were delivered to Northwest, an end of an era took place when the last DC-6B was removed from service May 20, 1965. The company inaugurated DC-6B service in December, 1953, on the Pacific Northwest-Hawaii route. Over the years, they had operated a total of 24 of the dependable Douglas 6Bs. Not forsaking the contribution of the noisy, complex piston-powered airliner's role in air commerce, the jet air transport was in its own unique league of ultimate passenger comfort, pilot acceptance and comparative simplicity of maintenance.

Ten Northwest captains honored by the Air Line Pilot's Association December 8, 1965, bid good luck and success to the swept-wing jets and retired with the venerable piston-engine aircraft. Honored at the Twin Cities banquet were Wilbur E. Morgan, who retired in May, 1964; Charles L. Wright (November, 1965), Paul C. Tarrant (November, 1964), Walter W. Wiencke (July, 1962), Henry L. Abbey (November, 1963), Carl Graf (October, 1965), Edwin C. Gunnerson (August, 1964), Glen Keepers (December, 1963), George Kruse (November, 1965), and Wayne Martin (July, 1962).

Northwest Airlines' all-jet fleet, now in the hands of younger but equally competent skippers, prepared to carry the company record of growth and achievement to even greater horizons.

DOUGLAS DC-8C

Northwest Airlines purchased five Douglas DC-8C intercontinental jet-liners shown above and below. The DC-8C, often referred to by pilots as the Cadillac of airliners, is capable of carrying up to 139 passengers at a 585 mph cruise speed. It is also capable of non-stop flights across the Pacific and return. The passenger cabin features two galleys and four lavatories. Captain Joe Kimm skippered Northwest's first DC-8 jet flight across the Pacific, Seattle-Tokyo in July, 1960. The first two DC-8s delivered to Northwest, N801US and N802US, were painted in older paint scheme; blue band on fuselage fore and aft above windows, with white NORTHWEST in band. N803US, N804US and N805US left the Santa Monica, California factory with new scheme: blue band incorporating windows, with blue NORTHWEST painted on white fuselage above the band as seen in photos; above, 804, and below, 803. Author's Note: All company numbers are now the same as aircraft registration number.

First scheduled jet through the Twin Cities was DC-8 (No. 802) shown above. Normally assigned to the Orient route, the DC-8 flight was flown from Seattle by supervisory personnel in January, 1961, during flight engineer's strike. Note older paint scheme which was updated as aircraft came in for overhaul. Robert Kuehn photo.

Northwest took another step into the jet age through the purchase of six Boeing 720B medium range jets. In above photo, the first unit of the order, N721US, nears completion for a scheduled July, 1961 delivery. The 720B, with its higher thrust Pratt & Whitney JT3D engines, can operate from short runways and has a reduced fuel consuption. The new jets offered more plane hours per day.

Above: With construction completed on Northwest's new general office building at Minneapolis-St. Paul International Airport, moving "day" was June, 1961. Moving operations performed by the Main Base Service department was an around-the-clock job which began June 15th. Moving days, for each department, were keyed to operations of the department. Norm Haglund, supervisor of the duplicating section, recalled in November, 1942, when he moved the entire duplicating department himself into the general office building at 1885 University Avenue, St. Paul. On June 22, 1961, when the department was moved, it consisted of eight staff members, presses, cutter, bindery equipment, photostatic equipment, cameras, darkroom equipment, plate-making machinery and various other components. Haglund joined others in applauding the new, spacious headquarters.

Crew of first jet into Miami were, from the top: Paul Littlefield, Alan Kirkpatrick, Ralph Render, Monty Leffel, unidentified, unidentified, Lalani Akana, Betty Baker, unidentified.

BOEING 720B

Delivery of the Boeing 720B medium range jets in mid-1961 enabled Northwest to expand greatly its pattern of jet service. The 623 mph Pratt & Whitney fan-powered airliners were first placed on the Twin Cities-Chicago and Twin Cities-Milwaukee-New York routes. The 720B, designated by the company as the backbone of its domestic fleet, originally carried 107 passengers in Northwest's configuartion. With an additional order of six 720Bs at a cost of $36,772,000, Northwest eventually operated 17 of the highly successful airliners. Above photo is of Northwest's first 720B, N721US. Below is N724US.

Right: Huge door of DC-7CF cargo plane allows loading of larger air freight items. The modified Douglas aircraft were used by Northwest on a once a week round-trip all-cargo service between New York and Tokyo. The new service, inaugurated September 30, 1961, also benefited Chicago, Seattle-Tacoma and Anchorage. It was the only through-plane, all-cargo service linking the eastern United States with the Orient. Northwest Airlines was an early pioneer in the fast growing air freight segment of air commerce.

In June, 1962, President Nyrop, shown at left with Boeing President William M. Allen, announced Northwest's purchase of three Boeing 707-320B long-range fanjets.

Right: Ready for business at New York's Idlewild International Airport is the spacious new terminal jointly occupied by Northwest Airlines, Northeast Airlines and Braniff International Airways. Building was dedicated and operations began November 18, 1962, in the $10 million unit terminal.

Above: Daily Waikiki visitor beginning December 15, 1962, was Northwest's fast, 720B fan-jets, operating on through, one-plane daily round trip schedule between New York and Honolulu, with stops en route at Chicago, Seattle-Tacoma and Portland.

Left: Northwest Airlines embarked on the most extensive promotion campaign on a single market in the company's history to sell its winter schedule to and from Florida. The October, 1962 announcement was made by Robert J. Wright, vice president-sales. The campaign, effective December, 1962, included: ten jet flights daily Chicago-Miami, six of which were non-stop; eight through jet trips daily, Twin Cities-Miami; three through jet flights daily, Milwaukee-Miami; two through jet services daily, Pacific Northwest-Miami; and jet flights serving Tampa, St. Petersburg and Atlanta, as well as Miami.

Above: Robert J. Wright has served as Northwest's vice president-sales since May 15, 1961. A native of Seattle, Wright attended the University of Washington and joined Northwest as a ticket agent in that city in 1946. From 1946-48, he was sales representative in Anchorage; 1948 he was asst. district sales manager, Washington, D.C. and Cleveland. That same year, he was the airline's first Hawaiian district sales manager. In 1950, he was district sales manager in Detroit until 1958, when he was named Twin Cities district sales manager. In 1960, he was appointed general sales manager.

Right: Graphic illustration of Northwest Airlines' Miami to Tokyo all-jet service.

BOEING 707-320B

Largest members of the Boeing "family of jets in 1962 were the 320 Intercontinentals, very long-range transports capable of carrying as many as 189 passengers. Northwest Airlines' first 320Bs went into service in mid-1963 on the Orient route. As the large fan-jet Boeings were integrated, they replaced the Douglas DC-8s, which were sold. In above photo is N353US, the third 320B delivered to the company, as it rotates on takeoff from Seattle-Tacoma International Airport. Below is N352US at Boeing's Renton plant. Employees in photo give viewer an idea of the hugeness of the aircraft. As of this writing, Northwest has operated 36 of the Boeing 320 B and C models.

Above: First Boeing 320B flight into Manila was skippered by Captain A. F. Antilla. First officer was J. A. Boom, D. A. Robertson was second officer and stewardesses were Sadako Kashikura and Yasuko Kobayashi. In October, 1963, Northwest inaugurated non-stop 320B service between Seattle-Tacoma and Tokyo; the first such flights to be scheduled from the U.S. coast to Japan. With the new schedule, the airline scored a jet-age milestone with the last DC-8 "straight" jets phased out of commercial service.

Below: Northwest's Boeing 720B fan-jet service extends to Atlanta, Georgia and the romantic deep South. Station manager at the time was L. J. Cash, who joined Northwest Airlines as a transportation agent at Chicago in November, 1945.

Right: Northwest's radio communications center in 1963 at its new general headquarters location. The facility, one of the most modern in the industry, plays an important role in coordinating many company operations, such as movement and location of aircraft, loading manifests and general company information. At left is radio operator Richard Brew, and in center of photo, veteran communicator Elroy Anderson.

Below: In keeping with jet-age air travel, spacious ultra-modern airport terminals were mandatory. In 1963, at Spokane, Washington, construction work was begun on a new $2 million terminal building with completion scheduled for early 1965. The new structure is being erected at Geiger Field.

145

BOEING 727-100

The return of the Trimotor. On February 24, 1964, Northwest Airlines announced the purchase of 11 Boeing 727-100 tri-jet airliners. The Buck Rogers type aircraft, with its high tailplane and fuselage mounted engines, were built by the Seattle-based aircraft firm founded on comprehensive studies of short-to-medium range airline operation requirements. Three fan-jet engines were chosen for reasons of economy and a maximum of power for short runway operations. Northwest's cabin configuration seated 93 passengers, who could cruise at 600+ mph with only a whisper of flight noise. As of this writing, Northwest has operated 55 Boeing tri-jets; the 727-100, 727C and 727-200 series. Above and below is N461US, the first 727 to be delivered to Northwest in November, 1964.

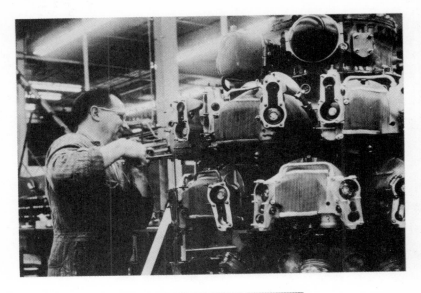

End of an era. Joe Smola, Main Base mechanic, installs final cylinder on last R-2800 piston engine to be overhauled in the engine shop. DC-6Bs, which are powered by the 2800s, are being phased out of Northwest's fleet.

Above: Northwest Airlines and UNIVAC officials sign a contract providing for installation of the airline's Twin Cities headquarters of a new UNIVAC 490 Real-Time computer system. In photo taken late in 1964 are, from left: L. E. Johnson, vice president of UNIVAC; E. A. Henson, UNIVAC Twin Cities branch area sales manager; P. L. Benscoter, Northwest vice president; and R. H. Weihe, Northwest director of communications.

Right: Northwest personnel get an advance look at UNIVAC 490 equipment, which is scheduled for March, 1965 operation to accommodate increased passenger reservations traffic. Anne Francis (center), Twin Cities reservation sales agent, and stewardess Marion Patterson, discuss operation of the new equipment with Patrick R. Smith, computer operator at UNIVAC's St. Paul plant.

Large (7' x 11') cargo door of one of Northwest's Boeing 320C long-range cargo-passenger airliners can be seen at left. The 320C retains all of the major systems and components of the 320B Intercontinental, but includes strengthened structural members to allow for heavier loading, plus the large door allowing easy handling of full-sized pallets. Convertibility to passenger or cargo configuration can be accomplished in a matter of hours. Boeing photo.

Right: Northwest employees load one of five pallets of computer equipment which cleared the Twin Cities for Tokyo aboard a 320C in June, 1965. Shipment totaled 28,000 pounds. Computer was waybilled to C. Itoh and Company, Osaka, for use in the firm's world-wide export-import business.

Left: Northwest employees slide pallet into position on floor bearings. Note floor-mounted binders used in keeping the load firmly secured.

148

Photo at right is of two Northwest Airlines' flight simulators at their Twin Cities training headquarters. The simulators, although very expensive, make possible checking-out and refresher operations of pilots far less costly than use of the actual aircraft. Simulator in foreground is for the 727 tri-jet airliners, while the one in the background is used for 707-320B and C models and 720B series.

Below: 727 prepares for winter takeoff at Minneapolis-St. Paul International Airport.

Spokane's new air terminal drew throngs of visitors at its dedication May 8, 1965, and on the following day. Several thousands walked through the Northwest 727 shown here, which was on display. In background is the distinctive central rotunda of the $2 million terminal building. George R. White was Northwest station manager at the time.

149

Chapter 9 — THE JUMBO JET

Northwest Airlines' astronomical equipment investments during their fleet modernization program of the early 1960's resulted in escalating net profits shortly after the fan-jet liners were placed in service. Since its record year of profits in 1964, the chain reaction of profitable operations, expanded and improved jet schedules, plus increased air travel, made 1965 another banner year for the company.

With the Boeing "family" of jets as their standard equipment, 727s served short-to-meduim routes. 720Bs on domestic trunk routes and key city non-stop flights, with the 320's for long-range Polar and Pacific flights to the Orient, the company enjoyed an unanticipated measure of aircraft utilization. In January, 1966, President Nyrop was quoted as saying, "...Public acceptance of these new and improved services has been gratifying. Northwest will continue to improve air service to the cities on its route structure by adding more jet airplanes to its present fleet ..."

A few months following his statement, President Nyrop announced Northwest as one of the earlier purchasers of the proposed Boeing giant jetliners designated the 747. The company, steadfastly endeavoring to operate the latest and best equipment with the ultimate of passenger comfort, placed an order for 15 of the new-concept aircraft at $21 million apiece, with scheduled delivery beginning in June, 1970.

The Boeing Company early 1960's research studies indicated a need for a high capacity, long-range, subsonic airliner to cope with passenger and cargo traffic of the 1970's. The

Opposite: The 747: Northwest Airlines flies into a new air age. The Boeing 747, first of the generation of super jets, was designed for air travelers of the 1970's. Weighing 355 tons, the jumbo-jet is longer than the Wright Brothers' first flight and the fuselage is almost twice as wide as the largest passenger plane then in service. The introduction of Boeing's billion dollar commercial gamble gave rise to descriptive names such as: Aluminum Overcast; Flying Whale; Fat Albert; and A Place in the Sky.

747, practically twice the size of the 707, was capable of carrying up to 490 passengers and afforded the opportunity for completely new interior and passenger accommodations.

As pioneer Northwest pilots and employees digested the concept of the huge Boeing, many recalled earlier career days, seemingly not too long ago, when the Ford Trimotor was a big airliner.

Further reflections and celebrations commemorated Northwest Airlines' 40th anniversary, which also marked its 20th year of flights to Anchorage, Alaska. Louis E. Koerner, veteran of 47 years in aviation, the last 37 of which were with Northwest, was qualified to observe the continuing spirit of cooperation and unity that had prevailed in the company the past four decades. Koerner was the most senior employee in point of service when a party was held honoring his retirement December 31, 1965.

Another very early-day pioneer aviator and airplane company operator, William A. Kidder, who helped Col. Brittin found Northwest Airways, contemplated the October 1st 40th anniversary. Octogenarian Kidder helped launch the company with a bucket of paint rather than the more traditional champagne, for he temporarily provided — after suitable repainting — two open cockpit biplanes with which Northwest inaugurated air mail service between the Twin Cities and Chicago on October 1, 1926.

October 1, 1966, the same day that Northwest observed their fortieth birthday and following a 15-year period of negotiations with the British government, a through-plane service began to Hong Kong. The new route sanction further enhanced Northwest's creditable Pacific stature. Additional stops of Osaka, Japan and Hilo, Hawaii were placed on the company's Pacific route system map on April 1 and

151

December, 1967, respectively. On May 15, 1968, Northwest Airlines personnel joined other aviation officials, government executives and representatives of the United States Post Office Department, commemorating the 50th anniversary of air mail. In the Twin Cities, Northwest pilot Dan Newman, Jr., became the center of attraction when he arrived at the celebration in his restored Waco J-5 biplane, similar to the aircraft Northwest Airways used in 1929. Post Office regional director Adrian P. Winkel handed Newman a sack of mail and as the circle of cameramen and reporters recorded the event, Newman climbed into the cockpit of his small plane and taxied down the ramp. The episode was symbolic of the "From Jenny to Jet" theme of the anniversary observance.

Another jet was in the planning of Northwest's future fleet when it was announced in January, 1969, that an order had been placed for 14 new long-range McDonnell-Douglas DC-10 tri-jet transports and options had been taken on an additional 14. The order made Northwest Airlines the first purchaser of the intercontinental DC-10, series 20, dubbed the "airbus" in aviation circles.

As the latest member of the famous Douglas line of DC airliners, the DC-10 offers a new dimension of comfort and convenience to air travelers because of its many improvements over the present generation of jet liners; more spacious cabin, larger seats, wider aisles, greater window area, lower cabin and sound levels and zoned air conditioning. Total cost for the initial 14 aircraft, scheduled for late 1972 delivery, is approximately $222 million.

Following this announcement, additional routes were awarded to Northwest, a recognized pioneer of Pacific operations. On August 1, 1969, the key San Francisco-Honolulu-Tokyo service was opened. Los Angeles was added as a second trans-Pacific-California terminal on January 6, 1970. With connecting service from the Twin Cities also inaugurated in 1969, Northwest had emerged as one of the world's leading trans-ocean long distance operators.

In June, 1969, the company kicked off its first trans-Atlantic flights when it inaugurated inter-change service between the Twin Cities and London with Pan American World Airways.

Northwest's new services and new aircraft had prompted a desire for a company "new look" designed for the fast-paced 1970's. President Nyrop's endeavor to reflect the best company image to the public, placed the important

assignment on the shoulders of the company's new asst. vice president-advertising, Britisher Bryan G. Moon, in March of 1968. The fastidious Moon, with the assistance of highly competent staffers, dug into the very roots of the company and methodically reconstructed it to reflect a truly modern jet-age image, not the least of which was Northwest Orient Airlines new logo and aircraft paint scheme. The 12-month task entailed in-depth studies, meetings with all echelons of the company and highly analytical ideas reflecting Northwest's leadership in world commercial aviation. The very effective result of the project earned Moon a full vice presidency and prestigious and economical benefits for Northwest.

As the new corporate image began to be implemented for the 1970's, Northwest Airlines' record of 44 years of continuous growth without benefit of a single merger appeared early in 1970 as though it might be broken. On November 11, 1969, proposals were announced which effectively would result in Northwest acquiring Northeast Airlines, with its valuable routes from New England to Florida and the Bahamas. The new merger plans were said to have more optimistic chances to materialize than did previous plans to merge with the late Capital Airlines, which failed in the early 1950's.

It was in the early fifties, 1954 to be exact, that former Northwest president Croil Hunter retired as chairman emeritus. Hunter, who joined Northwest in 1932 and expanded the company from a local carrier into a leading international airline, died in St. Paul on July 21, 1970. Aviation notables and thousands of government officials joined Northwest employees in mourning the passing of a great visionary and well-loved leader in commercial aviation.

On June 22, 1970, Northwest commenced its first 747 service between the Twin Cities and New York. Other cities to receive regularly scheduled 747 service as the jumbo jets were delivered were Chicago, Seattle, Miami, Los Angeles, San Francisco, Honolulu, Tokyo, Hong Kong, Manila and Anchorage.

A literal interpretation of the "Northwest Orient" incorporated in the gleaming new color scheme on a 747 fuselage in 1970 should not exclude one from believing that, regardless of the pending merger with Northeast Airlines, the Twin Cities airline is destined to expand to additional areas of global service as the company enters the 1970's.

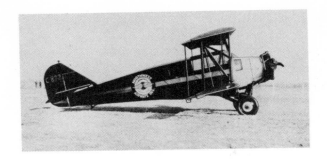

OCTOBER, 1966
N.W.A.
40TH ANNIVERSARY

Northwest Airlines' parade of aircraft, used in over 40 years of the company's history, is a panorama of the development of aviation. Beginning with photo above, and viewing clockwise: Stinson Detroiter, which went into service in 1926; Ford Trimotor, 1928; Lockheed Orion, fast plane of early 1934; Lockheed Electra, 1934, first modern airliner; Douglas DC-3, 1939, the plane that changed the world; Douglas DC-4, 1946, first of the four-engine airliners; Boeing Stratocuriser, 1949, first big air transport; Lockheed Constellation, 1954, fast, long-range aircraft; Lockheed Electra, 1959, first of the turboprop airliners; Douglas DC-8 (not shown), 1960, first straight jetliner; Boeing 720B, 320 B-C, first of fan-jet family; Boeing 727-100, 727C and 727-200, 1964, first tri-jets. Note: Also used by Northwest and not shown: Hamilton single-engine Metalplane, Waco biplanes, Lockheed Zephyrs, Martin 202, Douglas DC-6B and DC-7C.

Left: Up from the Ranks. Captain J. R. (Jack) Deveny, a native of South Dakota, began his Northwest career as an aircraft groomer in 1940. He became a master mechanic and then crew chief after serving his apprenticeship. Later, he became an air crew member as a flight engineer and soon graduated to first officer. In 1968, he moved to the left seat and his captaincy. As of this writing, Deveny skippers 727s out of the Twin Cities. His impressive Northwest record of achievement was interrupted only by a four-year hitch in the U.S. Navy during WW-II as a chief attached to the Naval Air Transport. Below is photo of decorative wall plaques representing each one of Northwest's emblems or logos. The handsome wood composite carvings were designed and made by Deveny's daughter, Kathleen Shuck. Kathy is an expert wood carver who decided that her dad would enjoy a set of carved wall plaques depicting the seven Northwest corporate symbols used by the airline. She presented them to her father as a Christmas present. Before the ecstatic Deveny could hang them in his den, fellow pilots and other employees began inquiring into the possiblity of obtaining a similar set. After months of searching, a firm was located that duplicates the original carvings in a high density polyurethane material.

Below: As Northwest Airlines developed into a major air carrier of the world in four decades of service. Minneapolis-St. Paul International Airport emerged as an important port of call on the world air map. Below is the airport's $10 million terminal building, a futuristic component of a $50 million Twin Cities airport development program. The terminal dedication on January 13, 1962, culminated a comprehensive program.

154

In keeping with jet age travel, new uniforms for Northwest stewardesses were announced in October, 1967. Modeling the new creations are, from the left: In Oriental jacket, Flora Dryer; Hawaiian muu muu, Karen Soderberg; winter uniform, Mimi Martin; VIP lounge jacket, Lee Winning.

Below: Northwest's new "Inta-Res" system, based on UNIVAC 494 computer, was installed at a cost of $24 million. The program system is operated at Northwest's Twin Cities general offices.

Above: Artist's conception of Northwest's Boeing 747, using outdated color scheme, was presented at the time of the company's order for 15 of the jumbo jets. The order, placed early in 1968, represented a total investment of $370 million.

Below: Mayor Richard Shoup of Missoula presents Certificate of Accomplishment to Missoula postmaster Guy Rogers in ceremonies held in that city on May 15, 1968, commemorating the 50th anniversary of air mail. Looking on, left to right: Bruce Vanica, Montana sales manager, George Burkhart, station manager, Robert Johnson, president of Johnson Flying Service and owner of Ford Trimotor (N7861), Mayor Shoup, postmaster Rogers, stewardess Donna D. Dahl, flight engineer Richard D. Frye, Captain Chuck W. Nichols, first officer John L. McKinnon and stewardess Carolyn "Kelly" Hight.

Above: Northwest receives Boeing's 707th 707. Three vice presidents showed up May 14, 1968, at Boeing's commercial delivery center in Seattle for delivery of the 707th four-engine Boeing jet liner. E. H. Boullioun, fourth from left, Boeing vice president and general manager of the company's commercial airplane division, delivered the 707-320's keys to Donald H. Hardesty, Northwest's vice president-finance. C. E. Dillion, third from left, Boeing vice president and manager of Renton Branch, which built the airplane, looks on. Two Boeing employees helped the Northwest crew, captained by Paul A. Soderlind, center, hold a sign proclaiming the event.

Northwest's first Boeing 727-200s. The first long-bodied 727s began service between the Twin Cities and Chicago on October 27, 1968. Boeing developed this stretched-out version of the highly successful tri-jet when it became apparent that certain airline routes had a need of a higher capacity, short-range jet transport. Northwest's first 727-200s carried 122 passengers and they have operated a total of 34 of the aircraft.

In-flight photo at left, snapped by a Northwest pilot, is a study of violent air turbulence conditions. A group of Northwest captains are contributing photos such as these to meteorology, endeavoring to assist them to a better understanding of rare and unusual atmospheric conditions conducive to air turbulence. Meteorologists are in turn better able to weather-brief all airline pilots to possible location and identifying features of turbulent areas, which then can be avoided to assure smoother and safer flights. Northwest skippers who have participated in the project are Captains Vince Doyle, Lloyd Milner, Cass Falenczykowski, O. D. Schroeder, Earle Perry, Ron McLaughlin and Ted Lieber.

Right: Beginning in January, 1969, a new in-flight magazine "Contrails" was placed aboard all Northwest airliners for passenger enlightenment while traveling Northwest. The publication was of bi-monthly issue. "Contrails" has since been renamed "Passages" and 150,000 copies are printed monthly for an available audience of over 800,000 monthly passengers.

Publications such as "Contrails" and "Passages" are an issue of Northwest Airlines' new (1969) outstanding vice president for public relations, Roy K. Erickson. A native of Minneapolis, Erickson was director of public relations for the J. L. Hudson Company of Detroit, one of the nation's largest department stores, before joining Northwest. A 1951 graduate of the University of Minnesota's journalism school, his early career was spent in newspaper reporting and editing in Ohio and Illinois.. Switching to public relations, Erickson served as executive secretary of the Minneapolis Aquatennial in 1956-57. A veteran who saw service both in the occupation forces in West Germany and during the Korean conflict, when not deeply engrossed in many and varied duties of his important staff position, he can usually be found practicing his No. 9 iron shot.

Early in 1969, Northwest Orient Airlines took on a new look for the fast paced 1970's. The idea was born in March, 1968, shortly after then assistant vice president for advertising Byran G. Moon came to Northwest. During the first six months, Moon reorganized Northwest's advertising literature and the tempo of the airline's advertising began to change. Ticket offices on the system were redesigned to reflect Northwest as the "big league" airline that it is. Later, Moon and his staff tackled the whole new look for the airline, including plane design and a new symbol, shown at left, designed by Clarence Lee of Clarence Lee Design, Honolulu. Others assisting Moon were freelance designer E. Williams Burke, Robert D. Blegen of Campbell-Mithun, Chicago, and Robert Wright, Northwest vice president-sales.

Left: Vice president-advertising Bryan G. Moon joined Northwest from Aloha Airlines, Hawaii, where he had served as assistant vice president-advertising, and public relations for two years. Prior to joining Aloha, he was director of advertising for the British Aircraft Corporation. Moon was born in Southampton, England, in 1927; graduated from Southampton College of Art and St. Mary's College. He is an elected member of the British Society of Aviation Artists. At the request of the author, Moon found time in his off-duty hours to design and lay out the handsome jacket of this book.

Northwest Airlines Skyshop, a simple and efficient "shop while you fly" mail order program, was added to the new look. Catalog shown at right, placed in each passenger seat aboard Northwest Airlines, offers the traveler a carefully selected range of travel accessories, souveniers and gifts which can be ordered with attached self-addressed, postage pre-paid order blank.

Above: Northwest placed an order for 14 McDonnell Douglas DC-10 luxury tri-jet transports in 1968. The order made Northwest the first buyer of the intercontinental DC-10 series 20, which is capable of non-stop flights of up to 4,900 statute miles with a full 268 passenger load. Total purchase price of the 14-ship package approximated $225 million. Delivery of the first DC-10 to Northwest is scheduled for mid-1972, with service inauguration slated for 1973 — the 70th anniversary of powered flight. McDonnell Douglas Corporation photo.

Below: Northwest Airlines' system-wide sales conference held in the Twin Cities in 1969 covered the airline's new image of the 1970's.

A Boeing 720B rolled into the Northwest Airlines' Twin Cities hangar in 1969 for a routine maintenance check and rolled out 60 hours later with dazzling new plumage. The aircraft, No. 721, and known as "Grandma," was the senior jet airliner of the company's jet fleet and became the first plane to be painted in the new paint scheme. "We anticipated a few minor problems in completing the first paint job," said Russ Ward, at the time Northwest's assistant district manager of maintenance. "The plane had to be stripped to bare metal, buffed, primed for the new polyurethane-base paint, masked, painted, and decals placed on the aircraft." While this beehive of activity was underway, continuing maintenance was being pulled at the same time.

Left: Employees on scaffolding remove paint from Northwest's famous red vertical fin while workman on stand performs maintenance on horizontal stabilizer.

Above: Ted Malaske, rear, and Dick Luehrs "boil off" the old paint from No. 721's fuselage with highly caustic paint remover.

Above: While the maintenance crew is eating lunch or on coffee break, the paint crew sprays "Grandma."

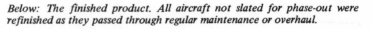

Below: The finished product. All aircraft not slated for phase-out were refinished as they passed through regular maintenance or overhaul.

Above: Boeing 720B, No. 727, undergoes a complete overhaul and refurbishing at Northwest's Twin Cities overhaul base. The airlines facilities, procedures and highly skilled personnel continue to be the envy of the industry. It has been said that the efficiency and split-second timing of overhaul equals having an extra jetliner in the fleet. The aircraft is completely inspected, inside and out. Engines are pulled as necessary and completely overhauled, honoring the latest modifications and manufacturer's bulletins. Interior compartments are refinished and redecorated befitting the current standard. When the bird emerges from the hangar, it is ready for another tour of safe, comfortable flights.

Northwest technician inspects "fan" of Pratt & Whitney JT3D turbofan jet engine. The impeller is restored to perfect balance following blade dressing and burnishing.

162

Outboard engine is reinstalled into wing-mounted nacelle cone. Prior to reinstallation, the engine and all its components are ground tested in a separate area, which includes a pneumatic facility that tests turbo compressors, turbine starters, cooling turbines and smaller units operated with compressed air.

Farings and cowling are installed. Note plug in engine intake, keeping out all foreign objects.

On the pre-flight line, another Northwest airliner is ready for service.

BOEING 747

On June 22, 1970, Northwest inaugurated Boeing 747 service between the Twin Cities and New York. Powered by four Pratt & Whitney JT9D turbofan engines, the spacious jet carries 362 passengers in Northwest Airlines' configuration, at a cruising speed of 625 mph. Both motion picture and audio programs are available for passenger enjoyment. Ten 747s and five 747Bs are currently in service. Above is Ship N601US, the first big Boeing delivered to Northwest April 30, 1970. Boeing photo.

Left: President Nyrop, left, and vice president-maintenance and engineering, Frank C. Judd, congratulate each other on the inauguration of the Boeing 747 service. The purchase price per aircraft was $21 million.

Flight crew members on first 747 Twin Cities-New York flight are, from the left, second officer Clarence Holter, first officer Harry Camm, and captain Warren Hempel. Ship No. 603 is in the background. The flight deck of a 747 is over 30 feet above the ground. The navigation system on the aircraft is smaller than an office file drawer, weighs about the same as a standard typewriter, yet can provide completely automatic guidance through any weather and to any point on earth with no outside radio contact.

A luxurious place in the sky. Resembling a modern hotel lobby, the spacious interior of the 747 offers a new experience in air travel. With a wide living room atmosphere, the main cabin is served by two fore and aft aisles and is divided by convenient lavatory and galley service modules. The flight deck, which is placed above the main cabin, has a large area aft which is accessible from below by a spiral staircase, and can be used for staterooms, a conference room or lounge. The freedom of passengers to move about creates for the first time a release from just sitting in a seat. A clockwise panorama of the Northwest jumbo jet begins with a photo at the top. (1) Welcome aboard a Northwest flight. (2) The finest cuisine aloft. (3) A relaxing first-class lounge. (4) A spacious, comfortable coach section. (5) Coach section lounge. (6) First-class section with all the amenities.

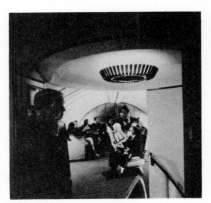

What it takes to dress an airline — The new Northwest look, left to right: Equipment service, ticket agent supervisor, ground hostess, purser, stewardess (summer white), stewardess (winter red), pilot, city ticket agent, mechanic and transportation agent.

In early 1970, a three-day conference was held in the Twin Cities outlining Northwest's new look. At the conference, new uniforms of Northwest employees for the 1970's were modeled. Attractive stewardesses, at right, model the winter red uniform, left, and summer white.

Left: The Twenties meets the Seventies — Waco biplane of the twenties beautifully restored by Northwest pilot Dan Newman, Jr. (in cockpit), is dramatically dwarfed by Boeing 747 jumbo jet. The Waco is similar to the aircraft that Northwest first put into service in 1929.

Croil Hunter, chairman emeritus of the board of Northwest Airlines, died July 21, 1970, in St. Paul. Hunter, 75, was president of the airline from 1937 to 1952. He served as board chairman until 1965 and is credited with putting the Twin Cities on the world air map. Under his management, Northwest was expanded from a local air mail carrier flying less than 400 miles into one of the world's top-ranking airlines, with a transcontinental, overseas and international network of more than 20,000 certified miles. Hunter was a native of Fargo, N.D. and was graduated from Yale University in 1915. From 1917 to 1919, he served as a captain in "F" Battery of the 338 Field Artillery, U.S. Army. From 1929 to 1932, he was manager of the New York office of First Bancraft Corp. He came with Northwest in 1932 as traffic manager and became vice president and general manager in 1933; president in 1937. In its long history, Northwest Airlines has had three distinct leaders.. Each was, and is, capable and successful in their own particular time period; the founding under Col. L.H. Brittin, the growth years with Croil Hunter and the survival with Donald Nyrop. Right: Bronze plaque recognizing Hunter's leadership is displayed in entrance ot the airline's Twin Cities training building.

The relative size of the Boeing 747 can be seen in above photo as a Northwest family of Boeing jets are being loaded at Minneapolis-St. Paul International Airport. In September, 1970, the airline took delivery of its sixth 747. Trans-Pacific service of the big Boeing was begun on July 1st with daily round-trips operating from New York to Chicago to Seattle and on to Tokyo. A weekly 747 trip was also being operated non-stop from Chicago to Honolulu and return. Early load factors had been outstanding since the newest jetliners were placed in service June 22, 1970.

Left: RENPA organized: At the suggestion of Northwest Captain Frank "Sam" Houston to form a Northwest retired pilot's club, a group of 30 pilots met May 28, 1970, at Seattle's Washington Plaza Hotel and voted unanimously to form the Retired Northwest Pilots Association (RENPA). Chartered in October, 1970, the elected officers were: Hal Barnes, Bellevue, Washington, president; Tom Hillis, Twin Cities, vice president-Minneapolis; Dudley Cox, Seattle, vice president-Seattle-Tacoma; C. W. Opsahl, Bellevue, Washington, secretary treasurer. Appointed to the board of directors were: Phil Bradshaw, Warren Shultz and C. Lee Wright. Merrill L. Kuehn was named vice president-Seattle-Tacoma, to fill the vacancy created by the death of Dudley Cox in November, 1971.

Northwest Captain Frank "Sam" Houston, who at this writing is skippering flights out of Seattle-Tacoma, hails from the "Big Sky Country" (Montana) and is the holder of WW-II Distinguished Flying Cross and various other medals. After piloting thirty B-17 missions over Germany and requesting 30 more, Houston found himself assigned to a top-secret mission dubbed "Aphrodite" — flying war-weary B-17 drone planes crammed with high explosives straight into German rocket launch sites in German-occupied France. Houston's role in this little known fantastic saga is published in Jack Olsen's book, Aphrodite: Desperate Mission, C. P. Putman's Sons (1970).

Left: First RENPA president, Captain Harold (Hal) Barnes, learned to fly in October, 1926, in Kokomo, Indiana, and graduated a second lieutenant pilot in the Army Air Corps in 1932. First flying for Northwest Novemeber 4, 1937, he was made captain in the spring of 1941. During WW-II, Barnes was a pilot of the 2nd Ferrying Group that flew the first fleet of Curtis C-46 transports to the China-Burma-India theater of operations. The group delivered desperately needed Burma airlift C-46s via South America-South Atlantic-Africa route. Later, Barnes flew military airlift on the Alaska-Aleutian routes of the northern region and test flew B-24-M Liberator bombers at Northwest's St. Paul modification center. Barnes, who is a former member of the Twin Cities famous 109th Aero Squadron, retired July 27, 1967. He has two unique flying distinctions: Early in his career, he flew a rare ornithopter (wing flapping) aircraft and, in 1960, while making a landing at Anchorage, his DC-7C hit two moose who suddenly darted on the runway directly into the path of the big Douglas. Barnes attempted to avoid the impending impact by pulling up from his touch-down but failing to do so, skillfully managed to make a perfect landing after the severe jolt of killing the two large animals. Fellow pilots enjoyed chiding Barnes for hunting out of season, hunting without a license and killing two moose with one projectile.

Above: Structural steel at Minneapolis-St. Paul airport forms a fitting backdrop for two Northwest Boeing 747 jetliners. When completed, the structures comprised two hangar facilities for the airline's 747 and Douglas DC-10 fleets.

Below: Northwest's new hangar facility erected in 1970 at Seattle-Tacoma International Airport, one of the airline's huge 747 maintenance bases. The $5½ million complex included an ultra-modern flight kitchen.

Right: At Northwest's Seattle-Tacoma flight kitchen, Helen Mabry and Mable Kuehl add finishing touches to delicious in-flight meals timed for immediate delivery to jetliner galleys of out-going flights. The airline maintains additional flight kitchens in Tokyo, Anchorage, Billings and the Twin Cities; they have been commended for the finest dietary meals in the industry.

Right: William F. Hochbrunn, Jr., Northwest's general manager of flight operations, demonstrates General Precision's GP-4 computer control panel, a component of the newly installed Boeing 747 flight simulator.

Below: The new $2.9 million 747 Lear flight simulator, installed in Northwest's new flight services building in the Twin Cities. The simulator training is combined with actual 747 training flights to aid in qualifying pilots on the new equipment. The total cost of all simulators and components far exceeds the total assets of Northwest Airlines in 1942.

Above: Shades of the past is this Link trainer used extensively by Northwest for pilot instrument training during the 1940's and 1950's. The Link trainer, invented by Edward Albert Link, first sold in 1929. By 1939, most air forces of the world and major airlines used the trainer. There is no doubt that they were the forerunners of today's complex flight simulators.

Long-time trainer operator of Northwest was Jerry Kimm, shown at left, adjusting simulator tracker. Kimm is the brother of Northwest captain Joe Kimm.

Right: Operator checks film projector used with 747 flight simulator. When operated by the pilot, the film gives him a visual reference to his manuevers. The film projection is coordinated with the movements of the massive trainer. Twenty hours of trainer time are required before continuing check-out in the actual 747 aircraft. Below is Robert M. Matta, Northwest director of flight training.

Right: Check pilot Robert C. Askeland is interviewed about his duties in Northwest's flight training program.

Left: Personnel attached to crew training center are (L-R) Glenn M. Anderson, Patricia Honsvall and Ralph Douglass. The training center is generally a beehive of activity as refresher and check-out schedules are met by the over 1,600 pilots of Northwest.

In photo at left is M. J. "Red" Costello, chief planner of flight dispatch. Below: Flight dispatch area or "bullpen."

Above: Northwest's Twin Cities large freight terminal, dock area. Below: Interior view. Air freight continues to enjoy tremendous growth as aircraft faster become larger and more powerful. Already, the Boeing all-cargo 747F, with drive-through loading and unloading by virtue of a hinged nose section, is capable of flying 100 tons in its 23,000 cubic feet of capacity. Northwest has kept pace with flying bulk items since the 1920's.

Above: Roland W. Chambers, Northwest assistant vice president-properties, indicates Northwest Airlines' future passenger loading area on mock-up of enlarged Seattle-Tacoma International Airport terminal facilities under construction in 1970. The multi-million dollar expansion program – one of the world's largest – is scheduled for completion late in 1972. Chambers, who has been deeply involved in many Northwest facilities expansions, came with the company in 1942 as a clerk based at Wold-Chamberlain Field. The South Dakota native graduated with an educational degree from Carlton College, Northfield, Minnesota, in 1937. During his career with the company, Chambers has held positions of superintendent of records, modification center; administrative assistant, travel-training; superintendent of cabin service, grooming; station manager at Washington, D.C. and the Twin Cities. In May, 1972, Chambers was promoted to full vice president-properties. Left: Northwest Seattle-Tacoma station manager George Harrison, left, inspects construction of modernized super-jet passenger terminal at Sea-Tac with Chambers.

With Northwest Airlines full fleet of fifteen 747s in operation, the company has been completely retuned and reorganized for the 1970's and continuing expansion. Destination — top of the ladder of success.

After leading the United States airline industry in net earnings for three consecutive years, Northwest Airlines slipped to second place in 1971. This was due, in part, to lingering effects of a lengthy strike in the last half of 1970. Loss of passenger and freight business to competition put the company in the red during the first half of 1971, but a very strong comeback during the last half of the year made possible the profitable performance for 1971.

Another factor in Northwest's failure to make four years in a row as number one in net profits was new competition on the airline routes. In 1970, the Civil Aeronatics Board certified additional air carriers on the direct Milwaukee-New York, the direct Twin Cities-New York and Twin Cities-Seattle-Portland routes. Early in 1971, an additional air carrier was certified over Northwest's routes from the Twin Cities to Florida.

All through 1971, the picture was disappointing and far from anticipated higher revenue. Northwest dug in to meet this new trend, overcome it and continue to keep pace and plan for tomorrow's business. The fleet modernization program continued with five new Model B 747s being delivered. The 747B jetliners are the longer-range version of the 747. As the additional jumbo jets joined the Northwest fleet, ten older aircraft were phased out and sold: Three Boeing 320s, three Boeing 720Bs and four Lockheed Electra turboprops.

One possibility of future business for the newest 747s lies in the resumption of service to China on routes granted to Northwest July 20, 1946. Scheduled stops at Peking, Nanking, Mukden, Harbin and Dairen were never inaugurated because of diplomatic relations with China and the United States. However, scheduled service to Shanghai was initiated in July, 1947, and continued for a two-year period. In 1948, the Shanghai route accounted for 30 per cent of the passenger miles on Northwest's international system.

With the opening up of preliminary relations between the United States and China, Northwest management advised the U.S. government that it was their intention to reinstate such service to the Asian mainland when conditions permit.

The management of Northwest had one bright spot in 1971 when, on May 20th, the company was cited in recognition of its programmed noise abatement project by the National Organization to Insure a Sound-Controlled Environment. Northwest had pioneered studies and implemented takeoff and landing procedures that would produce a minimum of noise without sacrifice of safety when passing over surrounding airport residential and business areas. The project was far from a miracle answer to the problem of noise at busy international airports, but Northwest was recognized for taking a big step in the right direction.

There was a miracle of modern flight in September, 1971, when a gray, tiger-striped cat named "Garfunkel" was retrieved from the vast inner structure of a Northwest 747. Approximately one month previous, Garfunkel left his Oshkosh, Wisconsin home to fly to Anchorage in the cargo suite. When the jumbo jet arrived at Anchorage and unloaded, the feline never got off the plane, for he had escaped from his cage in the giant cargo belly.

Garfunkel roamed mysteriously throughout the darkened no-man's land between the skin of the Boeing and the cabin lining, haunting maintenance men with its ghostly cries. Efforts to find Garfunkel or entice him out failed.

When the 747 was brought to Boeing's Paine Field in Everett, Washington, for scheduled modifications, the cargo crews discovered the cat was still alive and summoned Humane Society officials. Northwest officials estimated that Garfunkel had flown a million miles and were considering awarding a million-mile plaque; instead, they saw to the animal's recovery from malnutrition and dehydration and sent it to its owner in Anchorage on a red velvet pillow on the lap of stewardess Darlene Jevne.

Opposite: Stewardess Virginia Mundale, modeling the new mini-look uniform of red with knee high black boots and black shoulder bag, accentuates Northwest Airlines' new image of the super-jet age. Photo by Walter Hellman.

Late in 1971, an elusive stranger of another kind came aboard a Northwest jetliner and was soon to become synonymous with a new malady affecting world air industry — skyjacking.

On Thanksgiving eve, "D. B. Cooper" boarded Northwest Airlines' flight 305 at Portland, ticketed to Seattle. Twenty-eight minutes into the flight, Captain W. (Bill) Scott advised the FAA that he had a hijacker with an explosive device aboard. While the Northwest 727 flew a holding pattern 25 miles north of Seattle, officials gathered together $200,000 and a parachute demanded by "Cooper."

Two hours and 40 minutes after leaving Portland, Scott landed at Seattle-Tacoma. The money and parachute were put aboard and the passengers and two stewardesses were allowed to deplane. A third stewardess, Tina Mucklow, remained aboard as a hostage, along with the other three crew members. Yielding to demands of the hijacker, Scott took off from Seattle-Tacoma Airport with a flight plan filed for Reno, Nevada. Enroute, "D. B. Cooper" bailed out through the 727s tail loading ramp opening.

A rash of hijackings followed and drastic measures by airlines and government to curb the industrial disease increased.

In 1971, following the abandonment of the Northwest-Northeast merger, further efforts to a new merger between Northwest and Miami-based National Airlines intensified when agreement had been reached in principle to proceed with the plan. Stockholders of both firms approved the merger and hearings began January 25, 1972, before the Civil Aeronautics Board (CAB) examiner.

On May 22, 1972, the merger was rejected by the CAB examiner saying that, in his opinion, the merger was not needed for either financial or air service reasons and it would not be in the public interest. The entire matter will now go before the whole Civil Aeronautics Board.

Following this disheartening news, another event took place on June 30, 1972, when Northwest was struck by the Air Line Pilots Association.

Here we leave Northwest Airlines and their proud 46-year history — another cycle . . . progress . . . new equipment . . . new routes. But in 1976, when America celebrates its Bicentennial, Northwest Airlines will be flying faster, more comfortable DC-10 flights on its 50th anniversary.

A recent visitor to the McDonnell-Douglas DC-10 assembly facility in Long Beach was President Nyrop, shown here talking with Jackson R. McGowen, president of the Douglas Aircraft Company. In background is the first series 20 DC-10 aircraft which will be delivered to Northwest. The airline has 14 of the wide-bodied jetliners on order, the first of which is scheduled for late 1972 delivery. McDonnell-Douglas photo.

Three employees of the Northwest Airlines' Employees Credit Union received their 25-year award at Northwest's Service Award Banquet on October 23, 1971. They were Fred S. Smith, assistant treasurer, shown at left with Mrs. Smith; Mary McNeely, loan clerk, center, and Pete Patzke, treasurer-manager, shown with Mrs. Patzke. The credit union was founded in 1938.

It's all in the family when Northwest Airlines' Arnold clan reports for a flight on the Boeing 747. Captain Bill Arnold, left, first officer son Hazen Arnold and Hazen's new bride, stewardess Sheryl Arnold, have adjusted their schedules so they can make some flights together. As far as can be determined, this is a first for the company that three members of the same family have worked a Northwest flight. Portion of caption is a quote from the July 22, 1971 issue of the Edina Sun newspaper.

Left: Among the "firsts" which Northwest has recorded over its 46-year history was when the daughter of a former Northwest Airlines' stewardess herself became a stewardess with the company. Maureen "Mollie" Reiley, right, received her wings February 4, 1972, after completing training she began January 3, 1972, 33 years to the day after her mother, Kathleen Monsebroten Reiley, center, began her stewardess training in St. Paul. (See photo on page 66). Looking over Kathleen's scrapbook of her early days aboard the DC-3s is (L-R) Elaine Eisenhart, Marsha Robinson, Kathleen, Dave Reuter and Mollie.

Through the years, four members of the Bates family have shared in the growth of Northwest Airlines. Above 1928 photo is of Clarence Bates, who became a captain with Northwest in the early 1930's. Photo below is Janeau Bates, his wife, who started with the company as a Twin Cities reservation clerk after the death of her husband in a B-24 crash at Holman Field, October 31, 1942. She advanced to reservations supervisor before her death in 1951.

Left: Captain Robert C. Bates, son of Clarence, and his lovely stewardess wife, Janet, pause before their 747 flight for this photo. As a boy, Bates used to assist his father around the Northwest planes at Fargo, and always wanted to be a company pilot. He learned to fly at age 17 in early 1942, and earned his commercial rating before he graduated from high school. Joining Northwest as a co-pilot in 1943, Bates then flew briefly in the northern region before entering Naval flight training. After his release from military service, he rejoined Northwest and in 1949, earned his captaincy at age 24. He checked out in the 747 in February, 1971, and was based at Seattle-Tacoma before his untimely death in July, 1972.

Early in 1970, while Northwest Captain Vince Doyle was assisting the author on an earlier publication, plans were laid to document the history of Northwest Airlines. Largely through the unselfish efforts of Doyle, also company historian, many months of close association have been invested in preparing this colorful and fascinating airline story. In 1972 photo above, Doyle, left, and the author, check photos, captions and other material at Northwest's Twin Cities public relations department. Photo by Walter Hellman.

Left: Walter L. Hellman, a native of Boulder, Colorado, is manager of public relations for Northwest Airlines, stationed in the airline's Twin Cities general offices. After graduation from the University of Colorado with a degree in journalism, Hellman served four years in the Navy during the Korean conflict and then returned to complete his education under the G.I. bill. Later, he held the position of information officer for the U.S. National Park Service. He came to Northwest after nine years with the park service. Hellman extended every cooperation to the author in the preparation of this history. Gratitude is expressed also to Roy K. Erickson, vice president-public relations, and to secretary Carol Larson.

Here come the DC-10s: Massive wing section of the first Northwest DC-10 and the first series 20 is rolled out of the McDonnell-Douglas wing assembly area, headed for the final assembly building. McDonnell-Douglas photo.

Aft section of Northwest Airlines' first DC-10 series 20, registration number N141US, moves down the sub-assembly line toward final assembly floor. All photos page 182-183 courtesy of McDonnell-Douglas.

Center fuselage section is mated with wing root and forward fuselage section.

Inspection is made of Pratt & Whitney engine as part of complete pre-flight checkover.

Douglas crew for first flight of N141US (L-R) Joseph Tomich, John Chamberlain, Phil Blum, George Jansen and Henning Andresen.

First flight takeoff of N141US at Long Beach, California, February 28, 1972. The series 20 tri-jet gained altitude quickly as it headed out over the Pacific Ocean. It turned inland at a point north of Los Angeles and performed a series of prescribed tests before landing at Yuma, Arizona. Douglas test pilot George Jansen stated the ship flew better than anything he's had his hands on.

DOUGLAS DC-10

Delivery of Northwest's first Douglas DC-10 will be made in November, 1972. A total of 14 of the long-range series of this airplane were initially ordered which, with spare parts, represents a total investment of $290 million. In June, 1972, the company announced it was exercising options it held on eight DC-10s, increasing its order from 14 to 22. The newly ordered aircraft are scheduled for delivery in 1973, 1974 and 1975. Northwest configuration of the DC-10 can accommodate 200 economy class and 48 first-class passengers. Most aircraft systems on the aircraft will be provided with BITE — built-in test equipment — which will permit cockpit crew members to isolate and identify a malfunction while the aircraft is in flight. All of the new Douglas tri-jets will be powered by the Pratt & Whitney JT9D engine used in the company's 747B fleet, providing a commonality of engines. Above photo is of DC-10, N142US, the second "airbus" scheduled for Northwest delivery when flight tests are completed. Below: Another Northwest DC-10 rolls out of final assembly at Long Beach, California.

The tri-engine airplane of the 1920's meets the tri-engine of the 1970's. Douglas DC-10 (below), with its spacious interior and silent ride compared to Ford Trimotor (above), represents close to five decades of Northwest Airlines' progress. In 1928, the "Tin Goose" carried 14 passengers at a cruise speed of 85 mph. The wide bodied Douglas carries 248 passengers at 600 mph. The cost of one DC-10 would purchase 361 Fords in 1928. The fuselage of the Ford would easily fit into the eight-foot diameter duct of the DC-10's tail-mounted engine. On the eve of its golden aniversary, Northwest Airlines, the little airway that borrowed two airplanes to begin business, is busily planning for the late 1970's and 1980's.

AIRCRAFT APPENDIX

Northwest captain James W. Borden, who currently is based in the Twin Cities, was raised in Wadena, Minnesota. In 1944, he learned to fly in a 50 hp Piper J-3 Cub at Fergus Falls, Minnesota, and joined Northwest May 11, 1953. Borden is a recognized well-known authority on aircraft, aircraft engines, blueprints, photos and rare data in the airline and aircraft industries alike. He is compiling a publication that promises to be a "must" for aviation buffs and historians. Borden has unselfishly and enthusiastically assisted the author on many facets of Northwest Airlines' history and loaned rare photographs from his vast collection of meticulously filed prints. The following list of Northwest aircraft, compiled by Borden after years of painstaking research, is generously submitted for the reader's reference. Jack Deveny photo.

CURTISS "Oriole"
  Rented

THOMAS-MORSE "Scout"
  Rented

STINSON SB-1 "Detroiter"
  NWA No. 1 — C872
  NWA No. 2 - C873
  NWA No. 3 - C874
  NWA No. 4 - NC 2707

STINSON SM-2AB "Junior"
  NWA No. 15 - NC443H

HAMILTON H-45 "Metalplane"
  NWA No. 20 - C7523
  NWA No. 21 - C7791

HAMILTON H-47 "Metalplane"
  NWA No. 22 - NC537E
  NWA No. 23 - NC134E
  NWA No. 24 - NC558E
  NWA No. 25 - NC854E
  NWA No. 26 - NC69E
  NWA No. 27 - NC879H
  NWA No. 28 - NC7522

FORD 5-AT-A Trimotor
  NWA No. 30 - C7416
  NWA No. 31 - C7739

FORD 5-AT-C Trimotor
  NWA No. 32 - NC8410
  NWA No. 33 - NC8419

FORD 5-AT-B Trimotor
  NWA No. 34 - NC9676

WACO 10-9 GXE
  NWA No. (none) - C4774
  NWA No. (none) - C4775
  NWA No. (none) - C4776
  NWA No. (none) - C5274

WACO 1OW
  NWA No. 5 - C7446

WACO DSO-150
  NWA No. (none) - NC708E

WACO JTO
  NWA No. 7 - NR42M

WACO JYM
  NWA No. 6 - NR731K
  NWA No. 8 - NR631N

LAIRD LC "Commercial"
  NWA No. (none) - C240

LAIRD LC-R200 "Speedwing"
  NWA No. (none) - X7087
  (same ship as C240, converted)

SIKORSKY S38-B
  NWA No. 40 - NC303N

SIKORSKY S38-C
  NWA No. 41 - NC199H

TRAVELAIR A-6000-A
  NWA No. 45 - NC8704
  NWA No. 46 - NC9933
  NWA No. 47 - NC8122
  NWA No. 48 - NC ?

STEARMAN C3B
  NWA No. 9 - NC6255

FOKKER FIX "Super Universal"
  NWA No. (none) - NC341N

LOCKHEED 9D "Orion"
  NWA No. 50 - NC13747
  NWA No. 51 - NC13748
  NWA No. 52 - NC13749

LOCKHEED 10A "Electra"
  NWA No. 60 - NC233Y
  NWA No. 61 - NC14243
  NWA No. 62 - NC14244
  NWA No. 63 - NC14263
  NWA No. 64 - NC14260
  NWA No. 65 - NC14261
  NWA No. 66 - NC14262
  NWA No. 67 - NC14900
  NWA No. 68 - NC14907
  NWA No. 69 - NC14915
  NWA No. 70 - NC14934
  NWA No. 71 - NC14935
  NWA No. 72 - NC14936

LOCKHEED 10B "Electra"
  NWA No. 73 - NC14958

STINSON SR-5B "Reliant"
  NWA No. 10 - NC14170

STINSON SR-5C "Reliant"
  NWA No. 11 - NC13872

LOCKHEED 14H "Sky Zephyr"
NWA No. 82 - NC17382
NWA No. 83 - NC17383
NWA No. 84 - NC17384
NWA No. 85 - NC17385
NWA No. 86 - NC17386
NWA No. 87 - NC17387
NWA No. 88 - NC17388
NWA No. 89 - NC17389

LOCKHEED 14H2 "Sky Zephyr"
NWA No. 91 - NC17391
NWA No. 92 - NC17392
NWA No. 93 - NC17393
NWA No. 94- NC18994

STINSON SR-9D "Reliant"
NWA No. 36 - NC18429
Rented   NC17129

FAIRCHILD F-24-W-41
NWA No. 67 - NC15087
NWA No. 70 - NC16870

CESSNA UC-78 "Bobcat"
NWA No. 12 - NC50197

DOUGLAS DC-3
(Original ship no. in brackets)
NWA No. 301 (1) - NC21711
NWA No. 302 (2) - NC21712
NWA No. 303 (3) - NC21713
NWA No. 304 (4) - NC21714
NWA No. 305 (5) - NC21715
NWA No. 306 (6) - NC21716
NWA No. 307 (7) - NC21777
NWA No. 308 (8) - NC25608
NWA No. 309 (9) - NC25609
NWA No. 310 (10) - NC25610
NWA No. 321 - NC25621
NWA No. 322 - NC25622
NWA No. 323 - NC25623
NWA No. 324 - NC33324
NWA No. 325 - NC33325
NWA No. 326 - NC33326
NWA No. 327 - NC33327
NWA No. 328 - NC19928
NWA No. 329 - NC33329
NWA No. 331 - NC33331
NWA No. 332 - NC33332
NWA No. 333 - NC33333
NWA No. 334 - NC33334
NWA No. 335 - NC12935
NWA No. 336 - NC14236
NWA No. 337 - NC13437

NWA No. 339 - NC45339
NWA No. 344 - N39544
NWA No. 345 - N79056
NWA No. 346 - N19925
NWA No. 347 - N79055
NWA No. 348 - N17397
NWA No. 349 - N45333
NWA No. 350 - N12935
NWA No. 380 - N59409
NWA No. 381 - N28679

DOUGLAS DC-4
NWA No. 400 - N7900
NWA No. 401 - NX34538
NWA No. 402 - NC6402
NWA No. 403 - NC6403
NWA No. 404 - NC6404
NWA No. 407 - NC95407
NWA No. 408 - NC95408
NWA No. 411 - NC95411
NWA No. 412 - NC95412
NWA No. 413 - NC95413
NWA No. 414 - NC95414
NWA No. 415 - NC95415
NWA No. 416 - NC95416
NWA No. 419 - NC95419
NWA No. 420 - NC95420
NWA No. 421 - NC95421
NWA No. 422 - NC95422
NWA No. 423 - NC95423
NWA No. 424 - NC95424
NWA No. 425 - NC95425
NWA No. 426 - NC95426
NWA No. 427 - NC88785
NWA No. 428 - NC67067
NWA No. 429 - NC49529
NWA No. 430 - N88706
NWA No. 431 - N48762
NWA No. 432 - N68969
NWA No. 433 - N350E
NWA No. 434 - N88844
NWA No. 435 - N88818
NWA No. 452 - N88852
NWA No. 463 - N30063
NWA No. 473 - N37473
NWA No. 475 - N86575
NWA No. 479 - N42907

DOUGLAS DC-4 - Leased (Not repainted)
NWA No. 601 - N45342
NWA No. 607 - N34537
NWA No. 609 - N88709
NWA No. 617 - N88817
NWA No. 673 - N37473 (later purchased)
NWA No. 684 - N37684

MARTIN 202
NWA No. 537 - N93037
to and including
NWA No. 561 - N93061

BOEING B-377 "Stratocruiser"
NWA No. 701 - N74601
to and including
NWA No. 710 - N7461Q

DOUGLAS DC-6A
NWA No. 655 - N34955
NWA No. 656 - N34956
NWA No. 657 - N34957
NWA No. 658 - N34958
NWA No. 665 - N11565
NWA No. 666 - N566
NWA No. 671 - N571

DOUGLAS DC-6B
NWA No. 602 - N91302
NWA No. 604 - N91304
NWA No. 664 - N11564
NWA No. 667 - N567
NWA No. 668 - N568
NWA No. 669 - N569
NWA No. 670 - N570
NWA No. 672 - N572
NWA No. 673 - N573
NWA No. 674 - N574
NWA No. 675 - N575
NWA No. 676 - N576
NWA No. 677 - N577
NWA No. 678 - N578
NWA No. 679 - N579
NWA No. 681 - N581
NWA No. 682 - N582

LOCKHEED L-1049 "Constellation"
NWA No. 172 - N5172V
NWA No. 173 - N5173V
NWA No. 174 - N5174V
NWA No. 175 - N5175V

DOUBLAS DC-7C
NWA No. 281 - N2281
NWA No. 282 - N2282
NWA No. 283 - N2283
NWA No. 284 - N284
to and including
NWA No. 297 - N297

LOCKHEED L-188 "Electra"
NWA No. 121 - N121US
to and including
NWA No. 138 - N138US

DOUGLAS DC-8
NWA No. 801 - N801US
to and including
NWA No. 805 - N805US

BOEING 720-051B
NWA No. 721 - N721US
to and including
NWA No. 737 - N737US

BOEING 320B-1
NWA No. 351 - N351US
to and including
NWA No. 355 - N355US

BOEING 320B-2
NWA No. 377 - N377US
to and including
NWA No. 381 - N381US

BOEING 320C-3
NWA No. 356 - N356US
to and including
NWA No. 386 - N386US

BOEING 727-100
NWA No. 461 - N461US
to and including
NWA No. 480 - N480US

BOEING 727-C
NWA No. 488 - N488US
to and including
NWA No. 499 - N499US

BOEING 727-200
NWA No. 251 - N251US
to and including
NWA No. 274 - N274US

BOEING 747A
NWA No. 601 - N601US
to and including
NWA No. 610 - N610US

BOEING 747B
NWA No. 611 - N611US
to and including
NWA No. 615 - N615US

DOUBLAS DC-10 Series 20
NWA No. 141 - N141US
to and including
NWA No. 153 - N153US

BIBLIOGRAPHY

Published works

American Air Mail Society. *American Air Mail Catalogue*. vol. 2, 4th edition; Volume 3, 4th edition, Cinnaminson, N.J., 1969.

Boeing Company. *Pedigree of Champions: Boeing since 1916*. Seattle: Boeing Press, 1969.

Clark, Basil. *Polar Flight*. London: Ian Allen, 1964.

Clymer, Floyd. *From Jenny to Jet*: Pictorial Histories of the World's Great Airlines. New York: Bonanza Books, 1963.

Day, Beth. *Glacier Pilot*. The Story of Bob Reeve. New York: Holt, Rinehart and Winston, 1957.

Frederick, John H. *Commercial Air Transportation*. Chicago: Richard D. Irwin, Inc., 1942.

Garfield, Brian. *The Thousand-Mile War*: World War II in Alaska and the Aleutians. New York: Doubleday, 1969.

Ingells, Douglas J. *The Plane That Changed the World*: A biography of the DC-3. California: Aero Publishers, Inc., 1966.

Ingells, Douglas J. *Tin Goose*: The fabulous Ford Trimotor. California: Aero Publishers, Inc., 1968.

Johnson, George. *The Abominable Airlines*. New York: MacMillan, 1964.

LeMay, Gen. Curtis E. with McKinlay Kantor. *Mission with LeMay*. New York: Doubleday, 1965.

Lincke, Jack R. *Jenny Was No Lady*: The Story of the JN-4D. New York: W. W. Norton & Co., 1970.

Mason, Francis K. and Martin C. Windrow. *Air Facts and Feats*: A Record of Aerospace Achievement. New York: Doubleday, 1970.

Olsen, Jack. *Aphrodite: Desperate Mission*. New York: C. P. Putman's Sons, 1970.

Rhode, Bill. *Bailing Wire, Chewing Gum, and Guts*: The Story of the Gates Flying Circus. Port Washington, N.Y.: Kennikat Press, 1970.

Shrader, Welman A. *Fifty Years of Flight*: A Chronicle of the Aviation Industry in America. Cleveland, Ohio: Eaton Manufacturing Co., 1953.

Wood, Charles R. *Lines West*. Seattle: Superior, 1967.

World Book Encyclopedia, Field Enterprises Education Corporation, Chicago, Ill.

Periodicals

Aerospace Historian. Air Force Historical Foundation, Manhattan, Kan.

Air Classics. Challenge Publications, Inc. Canoga Park, Ca.

Air Progress. Petersen Publishing Co., Los Angeles, Ca.

Airlines Quarterly. Werner & Werner Corp., Santa Monica, Ca.

Airpower. Sentry Magazines, Inc., New York.

Alaska Industry. Anchorage, Ak.

Anchorage Times, Anchorage, Ak.

Dispatch-Pioneer Press, St. Paul, Minn.

Flying. Ziff-Davis Publishing Co., New York, N.Y.

Minneapolis Spokesman. Minneapolis, Minn.

Minneapolis Star and Tribune. Minneapolis, Minn.

Minnesota Flyer. Richfield, Minn.

Northwest Airlines Beam, News and Passage. Minneapolis, Minn.

Northwest Flyer. Tacoma, Wa.

OX-5 News, OX-5 Club of America, Pittsburgh, Pa.

Seattle Post Intelligencer, Seattle, Wa.

Seattle Times, Seattle, Wa.

Time: Weekly News Magazine, Time, Inc., New York.

Wings, Charter Communications, Inc., Granada Hills, Ca.

INDEX